FASHION, FASCISM & FEMINISM

FASHION, FASCISM & FEMINISM

The Collected Writings of Clotilde Desjardins Russell

CLOTILDE DESJARDINS RUSSELL

Sea Spray Books

Contents

FOREWORD

1	April 1939 - London	4
2	May 1939 - Paris	10
3	May 1939 - South of France	15
4	May 1939 - Budapest	21
5	May 1939 - Arrival in Bulgaria	27
6	May 1939 - Sofia, Bulgaria	30
7	September 1943 - Eulogy for Boris III	44
8	Some Spies I Have Known	54
9	The Contrabandier	57
10	April 1946 - Sailing on the Ile de France	61
11	May 1946 - Paris	69
12	May/June 1946 - South of France	82
13	July 1946 - Paris	105
14	July 1946 - London	123
15	April 1953 - Hail Women of Rio	131
16	1955 - Opportunities for Women of the Middle East	150

Foreword

Although I never really knew her, my paternal grandmother has always loomed large in my imagination. Clotilde Desjardins Russell died in 1970, when I was three years old, so I have only the vaguest memory of being taken to visit an old lady in shadowy rooms. A highly energetic and driven woman, the force of her personality stretches across time to me, perhaps because my father told me he saw similarities in our characters - not necessarily a flattering observation.

In sorting through my family papers, I came across many examples of her writing; travel diaries, essays, and speeches covering the years 1939-1955. They are a direct window into the experience of a woman who, as a travel companion to her peripatetic husband, had a singularly privileged view of significant twentieth-century events. Her primary interests were fashion and design, yet her awareness of broader developments, particularly nascent aspects of feminism, comes across in her writing. Whether marveling at the view from a hotel in Budapest or observing that Mr. Molotov resembled "a secretive little boy," her collection of essays has a clear place in my family book project and may serve as useful source material for anyone researching first-person historical narrative in the first half of the twentieth century. Where they exist, I have included photographs and postcards from our family archive. Where no photographic record exists, I have supplemented with images drawn from public, referenced, sources.

As I collated her writings, I was repeatedly struck by the way Chloe (as she called herself at the time of writing) seemed to walk into significant, yet seemingly fantastical events - whether the wedding of minor nobility in London, being particularly touched by one of the many tragic victims of Nazi annihilation, or witnessing the account of one of the heroines of "The Blitz" of London. In researching these people and events, I was often surprised to find that they truly existed and am glad that Chloe's experience has been preserved. In some cases, her language and perspective are dated or may seem inappropriate today, but I have left them unedited for historical accuracy.

In a fundamental way, my grandmother's writings are the heart of my family book project. The scars that her nature and behavior left on her children and grandchildren could have made it easier to leave her writings buried and unknown to later generations. As we better understand the nature of intergenerational trauma and epigenetics, I believe her writings worthy of preservation and choose to focus on her aesthetics and style - I think how she would prefer to be remembered.

Sarah E. Russell, September 2024

Clotilde Desjardins Russell as painted by Stanislav Rembski in 1932
Russell Family Estate

I

April 1939 - London

WFR's Passport Photo from the 1920's - It was not until later that Chloe had a passport of her own
Russell Family Archives

Editor's Introduction: From 1927 William F. Russell (WFR) held the position of Dean of Teacher's College, Columbia University. As a summer lecturer in the faculty of pedagogy at the Sorbonne, the family spent extended time in Paris every year. These annual trips to Europe continued until the eve of World War II.

London, Thursday April 27, 1939

Up at seven o'clock and out into the Green Park. The porters were washing the steps and sidewalks in St. James' Place and a woman with her coat hung on her shoulders walked ahead of me down the little narrow passage leading into the park. There the earth-works looking so yellow and clay-like and much unlike London are the first things one sees, but then away stretches the Green Park, long grass, chairs set out on the angle. Early London crossing from end to end on their spry way, walking to work.

A man with a small black spaniel was hunting for an owl. The owl has been hooting every night, so the man was trying to shoot the little nightly visitor. I am hoping he doesn't get him. There is no sound to equal the silent night in Duke's Hotel and the call of the owl or the air raid siren, simply all the noise that reaches that quiet spot.

Going on into St. James' Park the apple trees in blossom, the flower beds full of flowers, yellow first, then brown - straw flowers red, pink and white. Beds of tulips, beds or purple fluff balls, more flowering trees, laburnum, and on to the Serpentine where the ducks are being fed by the same people each day. On up the path to the steps leading to the Waterloo monument, past the Carlton House where the doorman with white cotton gloves in one hand, bends solicitously over a white rubber entrance mat and lays out a bit of cotton sheeting to maintain the spotlessness of the rubber for the awakening of the world.

Now into Lyons Corner House sitting in the cafe with a cup of coffee that the English say "will take some beating." And home again along St. James' Square where they are completely altering one of the big buildings, putting in a new interior. No building at home would be regarded as worthy of such extended repair, but the old buildings here are so solid and rich in substance that no one would dream of scrapping them.

Today I went to see the Museum of Sir John Soane next to Lincoln's Inn Fields. "Such a mixed up" as Alfonse would say.

The Dome over the Sarcophagus, with Sir Francis Chantrey's bust of Sir John Soane

Postcard from Russell Family Archives

An old Egyptian sarcophagus, scenes of Venice by Canaletto, Hogarth's Rake's Progress. Went from there to see Prince Henry's lovely old room, then home in pouring rain with just a bit of hail and plenty cold.

Will has been in bed all day suffering from the gout. Such an appropriate suffering for London. We cannot go to Paris for a few more days.

Friday April 28th, 1939

Up and out into the Green Park again. Yesterday's rain all is gone, and the sun is bright. Today Hitler is to make his long-delayed reply to the President's telegram. He had it written, ready to give last Tuesday. My idea is that he had waited to give his Navy time to arrive in the Mediterranean. Soon now the German Navy will be there in readiness to assist Mussolini. Then and if he makes his much-threatened seizure of Tunisia the reports from Rome are that there are now more Germans in Italy than Italians, and the Mediterranean has Italian, French, English and German battleships.

Yesterday a tale was told of the American ship Omaha on which American seamen were thrown into chains for thumbing their nose when the Italians gave the Mussolini salute. The authorities said the men were put in chains to keep them from causing trouble and that they were released when they arrived in Marseilles.

Later today extras were published containing Hitler's speech. Everyone seems to feel that he was very kind to England but sarcastic to the President. It is felt as far as people's comments go that he has right on his side. Much nervousness is shown in France. Jim has telephoned and written urging us not to come to France now.

The burning of the Paris, the burning of another troopship in Marseilles appears to be the work of people who do not want to be carried out of France to fight, the ships being burned maybe to destroy France's chance for sufficient numbers of men to take a stand In Tunisia.

Chloe with two of her three sons (Jim, left and Bob, right) at approximately the time of writing.
Russell Family Archives

Saturday, April 29, 1939

Up early and off into the Green Park for perhaps a last walk. The whole scene alive with footballers, some with guides, some alone. One of whom asked me, "What's down there?" Said I, "St. James' Palace", so he thanked me and set off to join his friends who were being treated to the tour of the outside by a man in a very dirty raincoat. Along the Serpentine hundreds of footballers were strolling in the only sun of the day, it being still short of eight o'clock. Many office workers were feeding the ducks and pigeons, and one woman was still sitting in her usual place, placidly smoking that strange sight, a pipe.

Last night in the restaurant, one woman sat alone in solitary grandeur. She sat and smoked while people were turned away again and again. She sat calmly and smoked four cigarettes before reluctantly releasing her place. At home I am sure she would have been asked to smoke elsewhere.

The hairdresser said England is still the only country in the world. She is Irish and wants never to see the place again. She loves London and says the Irish are witty but no Irish person cares for that. It takes the English to laugh and appreciate their wit. No Irish person will laugh at them but just say that they think they're smart!

At lunch one woman sitting behind me talking about Hitler. She said, "We've given him his chance in September, and now we've given him his last chance, so that is that"

I've taken Will to Sir John Soane's Museum. A man in his stocking feet let us in. He was a bit perturbed but kindly. "Are you from overseas?" he asked. Then he let us in.

Will limped around seeing the mirrors, the walls, slides and the fine old Canaletto, the Rake's Progress. What a marvelous man Soane must have been and what a place to spend many rainy days.

Now we're ready to leave for Paris. It has rained since noon. I stood out in front of the south entrance at Westminster and saw a wedding party arrive today.

A lovable English gathering. Men, women and children packed in every direction, talking to me as if I were not a stranger. Asking me who different guests were and so forth. One funny moment as a big Rolls Royce drew near the gate a familiar face showed through the windows and my neighbor nudged ne and said, "Who is he?" I said, "That's George Arliss" quite glibly as I'd seen it in the paper that George Arliss, Princess Elizabeth and so forth were due at the wedding. Everyone seemed to recognize him, and astounded whispers of "George Arliss" went the rounds. My neighbor gave a laugh, telling him he should be helpful and try to hold out a straw of something else for them to cling to now when all the world lives in an abyss of worry of what tomorrow may bring.

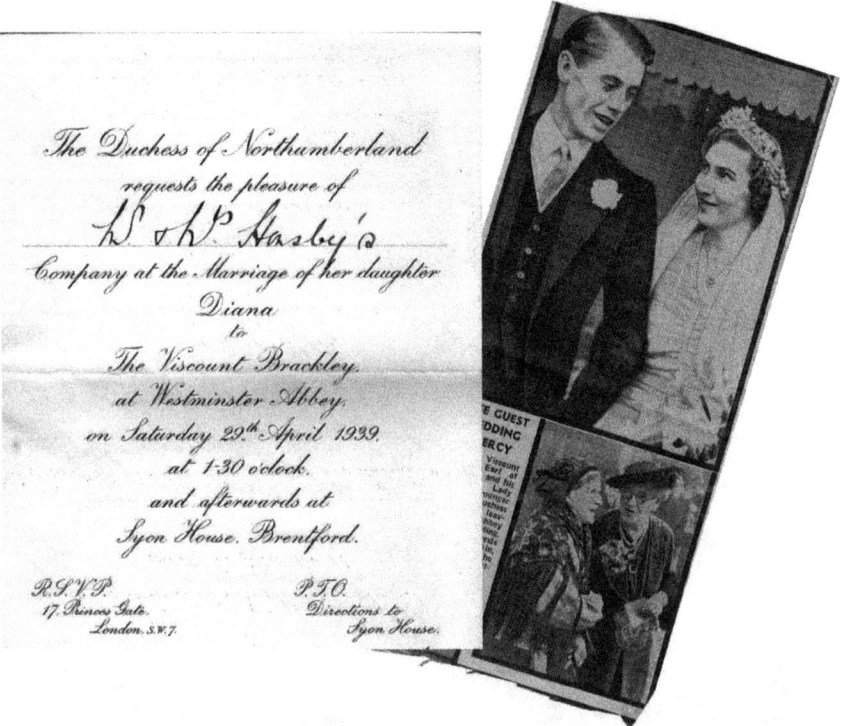

Chloe stumbled upon the wedding of Diana Percy to Viscount Brackley
Image credit: https://debatable-land/blogspot.com

2

May 1939 - Paris

Vintage postcard of Cafe de la Paix
Russell Family Archives

Paris, May 1, 1939

    Today I bought a fine suit for the trip and went to lunch at the Cafe de la Paix. It was crowded. The city is full of Americans. I find the French quiet and sad and very much improved in manners. The objectionable ones have gone from the public places and the raucous voice of the harridan can no longer be heard in the street. The hard, hideous-spirited hags that ran in all the streets rudely bumping and pushing one about have mysteriously vanished.

We visited Molyneaux for a brief bit of showing and then came home for tea. Jim was here with friends; Robert Barrat and one of his other friends, Madame Bompard and her granddaughter Marie. There were two very good jests.

There is a lovely garden on the roof of this building, and we went up there and saw the city before Madam and Marie left. Now they have gone to call on M. Bougle who is very ill.

May 2, 1939

Today they began work at 7 a.m. and we had more clanking of hammers on stone, deliveries of metal things. They are doing plumbing in the street, and we get the full benefit or those early morning efforts. The poor nightingales sing so exquisitely at night, but the plumbers completely rout the sylvan wood atmosphere when dawn arrives.

I feel sorry to see the pain and destruction caused by the Communists and now the Fascists bringing in a regime that was nothing like the French. The minions of Hitler are still here, and they are being well paid to sow their seeds of discord. The riot in September was engineered by them and I expect the poor French will once more be engineered by traitors into the next crisis. It is, however, now apparent that once more it may be, but not two times.

May 5, 1939

I waxed eloquent on non-political figures so to my surprise, Will walked in bearing a book autographed by Maurice Bedel. He had gone to call upon him. He told him how he enjoyed his works and was very warmly greeted and given his latest book. The book is called "Monsieur Hitler". I shall read it with pleasure.

Also, we have been invited to the celebration of the French Revolution out at Versailles. It was not possible to get three cards so Will rented a car, and we got the Brownells and started out, stopping first at the wonderful ___ for our lunch. It was a wonderful lunch.

> **CELEBRATION TO MARK FRENCH REVOLUTION**
>
> *Preparations Near Completion for 150th Anniversary*
>
> Wireless to THE NEW YORK TIMES.
>
> PARIS, April 22.—Preparations are about completed for a series of observances commemorating the 150th anniversary of the French Revolution to be held in Paris and other parts of France this year.
>
> The government has just decreed a credit of 15,000,000 francs, which will be expended chiefly on a celebration to be held on July 14 as the 150th anniversary of the fall of the Bastille.
>
> The series of fetes will open next week with a popular musical festival at the Salle Pleyel. This will be devoted to music and songs of the Revolution. On May 5 there will be important ceremonies at Versailles, including a special exhibit at the Versailles Museum commemorating the meeting of the States General held there.
>
> *New York Times Archive, April 22, 1939*

Chickens roasted over the blazing fire on the hearth for it was too cold to sit in the garden. We walked up the terraces and enjoyed the flowers and the pretty scenes from the porch and were contented.

We then went on to Versailles. A great number of police were out. We were sent round and around and finally stopped at the proper gate. We entered a place which once was once a great hall and now there is a huge tree in the center, so the hall has been demolished for these many years. The scene was laid out as it was at the time of the Estates-General. The tribune of dignitaries was set in the place that the King and the nobles had occupied before. Then in rows little plants, geraniums and greens were set out in the exact places of the third estate.

The affair was very simple. Souvenir programs were passed out. Not enough had been printed so half the audience got none. Everyone slunk into his place in the most democratic manner.

The President of France came skulking up from some sort of a basement and took his seat of honor in a very apologetic way.

Aerio (sp?) came in like a man, shaking hands and progressing to his seat with a certain amount of composure and appropriateness to his place of honor. The English Ambassador came in likewise and there was a handsome, bearded, colored man wearing a silk hat and gold hoops in his ears. He walked in with perfect poise and greeted the British Ambassador and others. He was undoubtedly some foreigner of distinction.

The program consisted of the President declaring it open and then with flowing golden hair and a silvery voice __ mounted to the second step on the dais in the center. There he stopped, standing neither up nor down and delivered a well... long, well-mouthed lot of poetry. When he finished M. Jean Zay, the Minister of Education, delivered a long address read in the best approved style of swoops and zoops. After that we all just got up and wandered out. Wandered hither and yon until we found our car. Then we drove up to the Chateau.

There we were herded into the Hall of Mirrors and one bit of charm and beauty relieved this dark democracy of everything. Drawn up before the Chateau were ___ and the engineers from the Ecole Polytechnic in their dress uniforms.

Inside the Chateau at intervals on the grand staircase they stood at attention with drawn swords. Some were in the uniforms of the territorials in white and red sashes, really fine.

When we arrived at Hall of Mirrors the mob was rushing. Chairs had been placed in the room, but the French women seized the chairs and rushed along striving to get as far toward the main point as possible. There a dais had been erected and red and white and blue bunting hung.

Seeing the lack of dignity produced such an unpleasant effect upon me, so we took chairs and seated ourselves at the back. One young man felt we had seated ourselves in the aisle, none existed of course, in any direction, so when the President entered humbly from a door on the dais and the audience rose, the young man seized my chair and pushed himself between me and Jim. The rest of the room was completely empty of people but that was the spot he chose. Jim seized the chair and replaced it in time as I had just started to reseat myself.

The President delivered a short address, then Aerio read an address in which he did his best to laud the idea of liberty, equality and fraternity but he was too honest. He faltered each time he said, "Liberté, Fraternité, Égalité".

To look about at that occasion, celebrating the revolution, was a very sad commentary upon the hideous example of a people who have killed their rulers, murdered countless women and children in cold blood solely because they were their betters and they were jealous of them.

France is paying now for that orgy of hate. The descendants of the revolutionaries are a sad lot.

Souvenir postcard from the 150th anniversary celebration of the French Revolution
Russell Family Archives

3

May 1939 - South of France

Editor's Introduction: Chloe and Will's eldest son, WFR Jr., suffered from severe asthma from a very young age. Driven to find a cure, Chloe brought him first to Lourdes and then to Cauterets, in the French Pyrenees. Cauterets is famous for its thermal springs, which were first in documented use under the Romans and are rich in sulphur, which is beneficial for auto-immune conditions - common complaints for the Desjardins-Russell family. The fortunate combination of altitude and healing waters brought relief and the region, and its people became dear to the family. Hiking in the mountains was a beloved family activity and they were all fond of their local guide, Jean-Marie Bordenave.

Lourdes, May 7, 1939.

We arrived here yesterday. It is like returning to heaven. The people are kind. The country is beautiful, the mountains near and the air is purified, all the political horrors are far away.

Thousands of pilgrims are here. This house is full of the English. When doors swing open, silk stockings are seen drying on towel bars. Shoes are in all the corridors and breakfast is served in the dining room.

We are most comfortable as we have a room with a big fireplace and two easy chairs. It makes a paradise for us. We go out and walk down to the grotto and get wet and then we come back to real comfort. We are having a beautiful time.

We drove up to Cauterets yesterday to have one of the baths, but we found the whole place locked up. It was open only on Sunday, so they closed it on Monday. The snow is so deep we cannot walk any place, so we are giving up that idea for the time being.

Postcard from Russell Family Archives

Today I was up early and went to the grotto in the pouring rain. The basilica was simply full. There must be about four thousand persons I should say.

We went to Tarbes for luncheon today. We had a marvelous lunch. A big trout, good piece of chicken and so forth. Monsieur Peyre was in the kitchen acting for one of his chefs who was ill. He invited us to the football finals. Will joined him but I came home.

We stopped at St. Savin to see Madam Jourly. Her little hotel as always neat and clean with its gorgeous view over the valley. All just as usual. She is gay and in good health in spite of the old monster who continues to maintain his "maitresse" - she who used to be the "cuisiniere."

Will went to Tarbes with M. Peyre. He first purchased some gifts for the babies. I suggested a little gold chain and a tiny cross and when he tried to buy a simple one without the "Jesu", great was the consternation! So, he carried two proper crucifixes to the little girls and great joy ensued. All the family gathered around to admire the one-year-old, who is encore coquette. She preened herself with her new necklace.

Monsieur Peyre then took Will out into the country where they entered the homes of the men who make the brandies. His description of the oak tables and cupboards and the cheerful fires burning on the hearth, all the comforts one associates with the historic days, is good. I wish he would write it up.

I've gone to the grotto many times always to find large crowds huddled everywhere praying aloud in unison in Dutch, Swiss or French. I find it distracting and destructive to my own ability to pray, used as I have been to silence, particularly at the crypt.

I marvel at this thing. It seems to me a union of souls and above everything seems to be the thought of war. The men are so serious and so devout. They drink the waters, carry flasks and pray aloud on their rosaries. There are innumerable ill ones. I helped a bit yesterday as there were too many for the volunteers to handle, so people from the side lines volunteered. I was supposed to say the rosary for my poor "malade" so she could make the responses but she was a Swiss and all I could do was pray silently. She did the same. I found the cart very heavy, and I was happy to deliver her safely to the guardian without mishap for I was terrified should I upset it.

Now it is Tuesday. A lovely bright, sunny morning. I went to early Mass but found "le monde" there before me, sick and all, hearing Mass in the bright sunshine. I met Will after Mass, and we sat in the sun in our little cafe and ate bread from the country, butter and radishes and drank the strange brew they now have in France which used to be coffee but now is a parched bit of grain with a little chicory added and a few beans of precious coffee to give it a hint.

We leave now for Cauterets where we hope to walk a bit in the mountains.

Cauterets, Wednesday, May 10, 1939.

We are here in the Hotel d'Angleterre. We have a beautiful room with a nice fireplace. We took it quite suddenly last night and drove to Lourdes and back in the pouring rain. We had the great pain and surprise of finding a stove had been installed in the beautiful fireplace. It was smoking most heartily into the room. We called them and made them take it out and leave the lovely fireplace free burning brightly.

We dined in solitary grandeur except for our waiter who is Spanish, blue-eyed and sympathetic. He told us all about the art works that were recovered in ___ having been carried out of Spain along with much gold by refugees on the Communist side. He said now all is finished. Poor Spain. To have to have a civil war in order for decent people to live and work in a decent way.

Hiking with Will and son Bob in the Pyrenees in the summer of 1937
Russell Family Archives

Today we had our "petit dejeuner", hot coffee, "pain grille" and excellent confiture made by the sister of the waiter. It is apple and pear, and last night the waiter insisted upon our tasting it.

We felt exactly like kings looking out on the hills, beholding before us our beautiful room all garnished above the mantelpiece with a French mirror and a gilded frame and a superb pair of candlesticks with five branches, and a beautiful old clock all made in Paris. The clock never will march again but how it is beautiful!

We have easy chairs and we have carried pieces of pine wood down off the road near the big avalanche on the way to the Pont du Gare. So many big pines are utterly matchwood now. The whole place smelled like Christmas. We came home bearing a sort of yule log on our backs, Will being very sarcastic about how I felt that all that hard labor was easy. We enjoyed our walk down from the Pont far more than going up. We were pretty tired when we arrived in front of the hotel.

Paris, May 13, 1939.
In Paris once more. We left Cauterets yesterday about nine in the morning. Our morning was a dream. The brilliant sun pouring in at the lovely windows, fire burning brightly, Spanish waiter with his blue eyes dancing came into the room exactly at seven thirty as he said he would and brought us our breakfast, "bien chaud".

We breakfasted and packed and left our charming home, but it was with deep regret.

The driver of the "Meilleure Taxi de Lourdes" was at the door. He is a nice man, polite and steady and careful. We asked we could leave Cauterets by the Mamelon Verte.

First, we went to see Jean-Marie who is to spend the day in bed for Will had hired him for the day and said what he wanted him to do was to rest and stay in bed. We took him some maps. Will found him in his bed with his wife taking care of him. Jean-Marie will be all right.

We drove out of town by the Mamelon Verte; a lovely view. Green, green grass, charming slopes, golden sunshine, poplars in delicate rows. The oxen plowing in the fields, the creamy cows so clean and well cared for. On down the gorge looking over Pierrefitte with its strange church tower. On down into the valley and there we watched the old Abbey of St. Sarin come into view on its eminence. Then the whole village bright and enticing against the side of the hill in full sunshine. The orange awning of Madame Jorly's hotel clearly indicating her perfect little gem of a terrace where one may sit and enjoy the panorama.

4

May 1939 - Budapest

Budapest, Tuesday May 15, 1939

And now we are in Budapest.

This room is perfect. Very high ceilings, spacious. Woodwork simple, all enameled in snowy white. The furniture is a shiny, light-colored mahogany. The beds are very comfortable and look so. They have big, soft, Alice-blue blankets and linen sheets with a quarter of an inch hem turned back, and two massive pillows - square to delight my heart. The carpet runs to the walls and is very floral, thick and clean. Our bath is enormous, white tiled and even has a wicker easy chair and a table covered with a lace doily. Lace doilies abound on the backs of easy chairs, on the dressers and on the tables. The windows are at least fifteen feet high and the curtains of lace and drapes of silk to match the carpet.

So, at last I've come to the best feature of this room, and it is the windows. One steps out onto a big balcony which overlooks the river and the view tonight of the bridge and the island and the lights and the river, which is silent and swiftly rushing by, the sidewalk, the cars speeding past and the innumerable cafes and beer gardens. I hear good orchestras playing La Traviata and we have had a grand cup of coffee with whipped cream and a cinnamon roll. Jim and I practiced our Hungarian and the waiter helped us to say it properly. We said, "Kucenom" and he said "Nichs meet". Jim and I were very happy because we had felt we were with sympathetic people.

The scene at the station with the porters who pushed our cart with our bags was very funny. One of the porters who was as big as they used to say "a pint of cider," looking for all the world like a dwarf from the Schwartzwald, dressed in a pale blue smock and stitched square shaped hat helped three other fellows, who were dressed the same, to push the truck with our bags. We came out into the place where all the old worn-out taxis in the world seemed to be drawn up. There was one chosen, and they heaped the bags into it, and we got in and drove home on the left side of the road.

Budapest, Wednesday May 16, 1939

We are sitting on our balcony. The sun is setting. All the world is walking up and down. The cafes are full. The lovely view of the river and the palace and the setting sun and the chatter of the people. Many officers walk with the rest of the world. They are big, stout men with dark trousers and khaki-colored jackets, cut squarely and with braided hats or caps with tapering toward the top. They carried swords. There were many children, but no dogs. How very nice, and what clean sidewalks. We are enjoying the officers, and their capes swing from their shoulders. They wear spotless white gloves with a sword in one hand and the lady friend is well dressed.

Budapest, Thursday May 18, 1939

Jim was up and out and gone when we left at 8 a.m. I stood on our balcony and waved our signal, but I don't think it was Jim I saw. We went to the Coronation Church for Mass as this is Ascension Day. It is only open once in a while. I was a little bit disappointed that there was no real affair. Just about three people and a low Mass. The high Mass will be at eleven. However, it was a beautiful old Gothic structure, and we were very happy to see it.

Budapest is perfectly beautiful. We came back to the hotel and breakfasted on the terrace. What a pleasure reading the papers from

London, all about Princesses Elizabeth and Margaret Rose going for their first trip on the underground. It was fun to hear how they sat with their eyes dancing and looked about.

We left here for a trip into the country. We drove up to the Dayack family home and picked up little Martha and found a lovely garden and a lovely home of black and white marble tiles on the floor and adorable furniture. Such a sweet family.

We proceeded to drive out into the country to see Boldog, a delightful place, very neat and a good little village with shining milk jugs on wooden pegs to show every house had a lot of good milk. Every house had its own well with a big wooden pole to work it, and here and there were clumps of locust or set out in spindly saplings over the whole place.

Every house had an overhanging roof making a nice veranda along one side. The house we entered was large and comfortable and very colorful, with a huge bed standing in one corner piled to the ceiling with goose down pillows covered in cases edged with

Vintage Postcard from Boldog
Russell Family Archives

what we call in English punchwork embroidery. I was prevailed upon to buy a few embroideries and a postal card. I was about to get one when one of the men in black clothes and hat expressed the wish that I take another one as his wife was the beauty shown there leaning over a small cradle in which reposed an incredibly tiny baby. Leaning over the baby in the attitude of loving mother was the handsome Hungarian woman in her organdy sleeves and peasant costume. Of course, we took the one with his wife in it.

Such a funny conversation with one of the guests at Mrs. Ackerson's luncheon. Baron Somebody. He was telling me of his experiences at the Opera in Budapest. He talked of ___ as if he had admired her and enjoyed her association very much. He talked of Lottie Lehmann saying, "too solid". He accompanied each word of description by the gestures of the arms indicating size and shape in generous sweeps. Then he began to tell how ___ was graceful and so beautiful from here to here pointing to his shoulder and then to his hip. Then he began to describe the hard time he had had.

He said, "she wouldn't let me go on but kept stopping me." "She wanted me way up here" and he pointed to his chest "instead of here" and he laid his hand on his heart. All the gestures and the accent accompanying it was very funny.

Then he told of the time he had been out to row alone in a boat with her. She was very strong he said, and rowing was her recreation - she used to go anytime taking her little dog. This time there was a terrible storm and a fisherman had to rescue her and row her home. As she was leaving the boat the fisherman attempted to help her land and the dog bit him to the horror of her troubled followers. However, he told how she gathered up the little dog and said, "Brave, brave. She saves my life." This to the dog and her followers had to pacify the fisherman.

"Well," said the little Baron, "she has about five little puppies, no wonder she wants to bite"

The Baron has a black, close-cropped mustache a square face and inky hair touched with gray. Grey eyes, very wide apart and he keeps them half shut His lower jaw is short and undershot. His upper jaw is prominent with wide spaced teeth. He speaks perfect English, is refined, intellectual and very pleasant.

A group of interesting people at the luncheon. Everyone is very accomplished. Mrs. Schuck has achieved such Hungarian that it is said of her that she is the first foreigner to really know the language. The Baron told me he is to receive his doctorate this fall. Mrs. Ackerson with her three children and all her duty seems to be able to entertain us, care for a sick sister and attend to all her other tasks. Her luncheon was delightful. Her home refreshing with Peruvian silver things. And a lovely portrait of her at great ease and beauty. That was an achievement. Her party for us was very agreeable.

(SRS Note: Garrett Ackerson was the last American diplomat to leave Budapest in 1940. His wife, Rhodita Ellen Edwards used the diplomatic immunity of their home to hide refugees fleeing Poland after WWII began in Sept. 1939[1])

Afterwards we went to the hotel and from there to the lecture at the House of Parliament where Dr. Cornish met us and escorted us up the stairs. A vivid, colorful, immensely high and imposing stairway with the ceiling all in mosaics, beams and rails and stairs leading in four ways from the center.

It was an experience to go up such a staircase and in his company with his gentle, slow way of going. His clothes and cloth shoes with patent leather tips, his black coat Prince Albert cut, his huge pock-scarred face and intelligent countenance gave a feeling of being in this historical place in the company of one who was truly great.

He introduced Will while sitting down reading his words. When Will was through he began to thank him in a little prepared statement but warmed up to the subject and gave him a really affectionate and glowing tribute as he ended. I was in tears as Will had been very good. When he began to quote from ____. I felt myself getting hysterical.

We have had dinner with Dr. Bodash. He had such a beautiful party for us. His apartment is comfortable. We arrived at the train early and now are sitting waiting in the station while the trains let off steam with the noises of all railway stations.

We went into a large apartment house, entered through wrought iron gates. There was a little man in a cap who came out and escorted us to the elevator and announced that only two could enter at one time. Will and I entered. I couldn't think in Hungarian how I should say thank you to him. I remembered "P___ and S___." Then as we went in and slowly began climbing, I began to think of other Hungarian words. What was the difference for instance between good evening and "__"

and "how do you do?" So, in practicing, I said to my husband "you see good evening is "___"

I intended to go on with the rest of my thoughts when the little man running the elevator gravely lifted his cap and turned to me and said "___" and went on slowly with us to the top. Will's face was a study. When we stepped out, he could bear it no longer and we both laughed. He said he felt that showed my ability.

When we went to ring the doorbell, it rebounded with such a loud peal, and we were admitted by a pleasant young man and had a perfectly delightful evening.

---

[1] *Daniels, Lee. Garret Ackerson Obituary, New York Times, September 16, 1992, p.25*

5

May 1939 - Arrival in Bulgaria

Editor's Introduction: In May 1939, the University of Sofia celebrated its 50th anniversary and academic dignitaries from around the world were invited to participate. WFR was nominated from the US, possibly also as a result of his intelligence connections.

Yugoslavia-Bulgaria, Saturday, May 20, 1939

We left Belgrade a short time ago and are now crossing Yugoslavia. It is wild and much like the country around Boldog. There are many animals. Sheep with long coats, and pigs and cows and go forth. I saw seven women and two men working in the fields all in a row the way they work the beet fields in Colorado. One woman and a little girl tending cows had a huge bunch of wool on her staff and was spinning her thread as she tended her animals. The men looked so picturesque with khaki suits, thick leggings and square caps.

Going down to Sophia on the Orient Express, when on the way to the diner, we found a large man stationed in the passage. We all had to squeeze past him, and he did not stir. This proved to be the servant of a large elegantly dressed man who occupied the room next to ours. He stared at us through his monocle.

Passengers said in my hearing, "There aren't many of that type left. That fine old gentleman is of the old-style good Germans." "Well, it is an old saying, is it not, like servant, like man?", "I would like to punch his ugly mug" "These Germans are so cocky, what makes them that way?" "Oh, don't you remember? The Master Race!"

We noticed with little enthusiasm, that when we arrived these Germans stepped off the train also and were welcomed by a party of friends. We were met officially as we were the guests of the country at the celebration of the fiftieth anniversary of the founding of the modern University of Bulgaria.

Coming into the station we were met by a delegation of Mrs. Omarschefsky carrying a bunch of roses and her son, and Mr. Omarschefsky and Mr. Peerwitz and Miss Cassanova. We were made to stand in a row for a picture. So of all things, I'm standing there with eyes cocked on heaven as if I had just smelled my roses and found them divine.

The silly thing I did was to look up to see if the flag of the U.S.A. was flying from the roof as were the ones of the other nations. It was not, but American flag at the Embassy was enormous.

When we arrived in Sofia, we rode up to the hotel in a big automobile with the Omarschefskys, Miss Cassanova and Mr. Peerwitz and were stopped by the police and made to descend and walk the rest of the way into the hotel. The entrance was around the corner so as we followed the curve of the road, we found a squadron of horse guards drawn up before our hotel. Very Bulgarian in round caps with short visors, khaki suits and long swords in hand.

Suddenly ___ came out of the Palace gates and rolled up before the entrance. It was an open landau drawn by horses and the two men seated in it were the Minister of Foreign Affairs and the new Polish Minister.

It was a colorful introduction to Sofia. We were thoroughly welcomed and helped in every way. We felt very much at home.

It developed that it being Saturday night, Sunday would be the time when no pressing could be done so if there was any pressing needed, we must have it done immediately. Miss Cassanova had made arrangements for her cook to come, bringing her American electric iron and ironing all of our things here on the desk. The cook was working away when I came in. I was much interested in her appearance.

She was very short, dressed in black with a dark scarf over her head, perfectly tight and hanging to one side in back. As she ironed away, her back to me, I was amazed to see a long braid of grey hair hanging down her back under the scarf.

Later I grew accustomed to that oddity. It is the style of a certain group in Bulgaria. She wound up the braid and the scarf around her head when she was ready to go later and looked very neat. She speaks French in a very smooth voice. I was much impressed by her. Miss Cassanova said she had two children both doing their service in the Army for which wages are very low. The oldest son is 27 and he has six children. Being the grandmother, she is working hard to support them while the father is away.

As for Sofia - the impressions on arriving are that one is now in the East. It is a modern city, not too busy or humming. One sees lovely vistas of the mountains. The streets are sometimes paved in a light-yellow brick and quite slippery. The children run and glide when crossing them and the little thin horses drawing the droshkies slip as they run lightly over the bricks. One hears the traffic of Sofia as a clicking on the bricks and automobile horns. Every evening about five the entire populace comes out to walk. The King has given the city a lovely park. It belongs only to the children. No grown-ups can enter unless in care of a child. A favorite place to walk is from the Palace to the park and how they do walk! The students in their caps, in bands weaving in out, everyone in their smartest hat out to see and be seen.

6

May 1939 - Sofia, Bulgaria

Sofia, Sunday May 21, 1939

We awakened at about six and a cool breeze blew in from the mountains. I closed the big windows and drew the curtains and then we slept on till eight. We had our café au lait and magnificent cherry jam, honey and marmalade.

I concentrated on the jam which was extremely good. The bread had strong cellophane leanings so I suppose they sell the wheat to Germany and use some form of substitute.

WFR's decorations - small size
Russell Family Estate

We dressed and Will put on his decorations (The French Legion d'Honneur 2nd Class and Serbian order of St Sava) looking perfectly magnificent wearing his white tie and tails and silk hat. Jim in his tails also and opera hat. They fared forth and when I saw them next it was in the procession coming into the church where we were attending the ceremony.

Large Bishops, four of them, with full beards and crowns of pierced metal were officiating. The service was very impressive and the voices of the priests and their chants perfectly glorious. The choir also.

The people were from all of Europe. About 60 fine looking German men and their wives. 25 or 30 Italians and 15 French and about 15 English - 6 Americans. A good-looking gathering.

We went to the University after the ceremony. And there the greetings from the colleges and universities were delivered. First a handsome Bulgar dressed in a big black velvet hat and black gown took a stand on the platform, holding a huge ___. The students' choir standing in the balcony all dressed in white caps and cotton red embroidered shirts began cheering and the King and Queen came in.

The choir sang the national anthem in full voice.

The director, a charming, dark-eyed, handsome Bulgarian started the proceedings. After two speeches of welcome the Delegates began to present their greetings.

First, a fine-looking, bald German greeted the University and made a gift of 1,000 volumes for the library. Roars of applause and cheers. Nazi salutes. The academic robes of Germany are particularly fine. One is a plain black with borders and gloves of scarlet. Another with a white Elizabethan ruff. Another a lovely emerald green with a round collarette and a square cap of green velvet. Another of deep blue velvet with a high-standing collar and border and a white tucker of linen. The Germans made gifts of huge portfolios of tooled leather and parchment in tubes and finally gave two other honorary degrees to the members of the University who had made their studies in Germany and amongst those were the Rector.

The German who presented them spoke in a clear loud voice, a fine-looking man, clever and polite. All in all, Germany has sent not only their most distinguished scholars, but their handsomest, most polished men as well as women. The women are gorgeously gowned. They appear to be of the highest class.

The Italians are also a fine group. Tall and handsome.

The Swedish lady, Mrs. Hogquist, I had met and liked very much. She said, "I've been in Germany many times and I know the Germans are handsome and very clever, but I thought the Italians were short and ugly and I find them just as fine as the Germans."

They were indeed, and saluting abruptly, the palm or hand with the gorgeous old robes of velvet, etc. Mink capes hanging to the waist. Ermine collarettes hanging to their elbows. Decorations, medals and sleeves lined in cerise turned out for the full picturesque effect as the salute is given.

I for one have been simply dazzled.

The English have Lord Percy. He appeared in full regalia with an enormous gown of silk with a collarette of sliver galleon. He delivered his greetings in French very well.

The other English gave gifts as well and wore their traditional university caps and gowns with full swank.

Will presented the greetings from the U.S.A. As he said, "From the youngest culture to the oldest". He was wearing full dress with his cross of Saint Cyril/Sava on his breast and his rosette and medal of the Legion d'Honneur on his breast pocket.

WFR's Legion d'Honneur decoration - large size
Russell Family Estate

He took plenty of time, bowed to the King and then to the Queen and bowed to the audience, addressed their Majesties and the audience. He was never in better voice or manner. We were all gratified when the Queen called a girl who is in charge of nurses in a charity in which she is interested and sent her round to call on us and thank Will for the references to Saints Cyril, Methodius and Simeon and ___.

Upon leaving we preceded down the street between rows or poplars. As we went along, we were applauded. The Germans and Italians threw up their hands in their salute, but Will and Jim just now and then lifted the tall hat.

Sofia, Monday May 22, 1939

We went to visit a girls' school, but as we had to go home to dress for a visit to the King, we soon began a long leave-taking making speeches, being given presents and with very much laughing. I was given a lovely bright green native apron which I declared was the most perfect gift as it matched the leaves on my white hat. Jim was given a teacloth, embroidered, with the words that now he was ready to marry, and he needs a teacloth. That came as the result of this little experience:

Will had taken out his pipe. Mr. ___ came forth to light it for him. He carried a sort of tobacco pouch. He drew from it a piece or moss, kind of a sponge-like substance and then a piece of flint like an arrowhead and he struck the steel on the flint and held it against a piece of sponge pulled from the large piece. He gave it to Will who put it in his pipe, drew and it began to smoke. Then the apparatus was passed to all of us, and it ended up with Jim, who taking it tried it and struck a light. Everyone began to chatter in Bulgarian and it came out that when a young man can do that, he is ready to marry.

So now he has his teacloth and is ready to begin housekeeping.

We finally left and returned to the hotel and there dressed in our best. While in Paris, knowing I'd need to look my best in Sofia I went to Premet and got a very good new suit - it was a pale shade, a sort of cross between a pink and a lavender and was made with a short loose jacket. Around the neck and down each side of the front was a band of fluffed otter. The skirt has a few pleats in front and in back, so it looks graceful as one moves. I wore with it a light blue chiffon blouse made by Louise ___, entirely covered with small, stitched box pleats with a little standing collar with a bow in front and short sleeves. My hat is an exact match to the suit and comes from le M___. My bag matches the fur and my shoes. It was a good-looking outfit, I feel.

The German delegation always waited until I came down and then they came out on the sidewalks and exhibited before the crowd right with me until I felt sure the crowd thought "Oh she's German". Try as we would we could not evade them and when we went to the Palace we tried slowing up and all the known tricks but we were obliged to advance before all Sofia with the handsome Germans exactly beside Jim, Will and me.

Standing in line at the Palace once more we were surrounded but our Minister was finally able to pry us loose. Then we passed in between various dignitaries leaving the men's hats and gloves and with Jim, Will and I leading the way, we all mounted stairs.

The landings were banked with flowers, some the loveliest. At the head of the stairs one huge decoration at the base of an enormous mirror. It was of large, deep peonies and ferns; I was impressed with the variety and beauty of the flowers and the artistic arrangement of them throughout the visit.

We were greeted on the stairs by the protocol man. He kindly went up with us. We were received by the lady-in-waiting and the King's sister who were speaking English. We were then shown into the salon and told where to stand. We had a favored spot with our backs to the light where we could see everything. It is well the Germans are trained and disciplined as they couldn't see a single thing.

Finally, everyone had arrived. There was a number all the way around the room, our Minister looking very nice as always and very kind and gracious and introduced us when the King came. The husbands and wives together. We stood in a little band. Will and I first, Mr. and Mrs. Black second, and Mr. and Mrs. van Valkenberg third, Jim and Mr. Bliss fourth. Mr. van Valkenberg said, "There are 97 Germans here. What is the matter with a nation that needs to send that many?" We are a small number but classy, so we felt.

The musicians shortly struck up the King's hymn and his Royal Highness arrived. He proceeded swiftly around the room shaking hands with each of us. Then we were told to go into the refreshment rooms where large tables were laid out with a generous supply of tea things. Strawberries are a specialty of Sofia and there were dishes of large strawberries all in uniform size, all with the stem cut just the same length so one held it by stem quite firmly in order to eat it.

There were trays of drinks passed, cups or hot tea or fruit juices and later on glasses of champagne. The strawberries were in compotes and there were cakes and candies galore. It was a regal spread.

As we went into the other rooms the doors of the grand salon were closed and opened later. Each table stood down the middle of the room laden with flowers and good things. The crystal chandeliers were all alight.

Finally, we were told by Mr. Atherton to be ready to have a private talk with the Queen, so we stood with him at the door until we were summoned. And then we went into the rooms where she was sitting. She's a charming girl, very intelligent and amiable and pretty. Her eyes are a light brown. She has a delightful way of speaking English and a sweet voice and a gay and vivacious way.

She was dressed in a very good-looking yellow dress of undotted chic and a fine cape of mink. She had me beside her on the sofa and we each had a short visit with her. She questioned me, asking various questions - finally getting on to ships. "How would I go home?" Asking me if I liked it - if I'd sailed on the Queen Mary etc., etc. We all had to laugh afterwards as I told her how nice the Normandy is and asked her if she liked ships. She said, "No." And I said, "Well, the Normandy is more like a huge, first-class modern hotel and so on." Mr. Atherton said, "But Madam they can go to New York just as fast on the ___ and she is a fine ship. I know as I've traveled on her." So on and so on. Afterwards we laughed and thanked him for saving the day so tactfully.

In the room were flowers on the mantelpiece hanging to the floor from huge vases. Sweet pea vines and brilliant pink geraniums, all very interesting and unusual looking.

We emerged and from then prepared to leave. Suddenly Mr. Atherton appeared again saying, "No, don't go. You can't go after all." So, we remained waiting for the signal and finally it came – the King arrived. He went from group to group taking plenty of time and chatting in an animated way. Finally, he came up to Will and began to talk. Shortly Will turned and called Jim who came up. He and the King began to talk in French. Then Will called me and we all had a nice talk. Then Will called the Blacks, Miss Turner and Mr. Manning, Mr. Bliss and Mr vanValkenberg. We all had a nice talk and enjoyed it.

The King is very gentle, with a high nose and blue, intelligent, merry eyes. His way seems to be witty and bright. He enjoyed our remarks and seemed easy to talk with and put us entirely at our ease. People seemed to love him, and it was easy to see why.

One of the delegates had been an Indian. He wears a fez and a long black tunic. One of the men said of a lady from the Belgian legation who was wearing a very smart white turban. "Is she the wife of the man in the fez?" This was very funny to us all. I seem to have said my say to some reporter as Mr. Omarschefsky called our attention to a bit in the paper where I said I found everything very nice. I'm so glad since without knowing it, I had spoken to a reporter, and I had said what I felt and that everything was very nice indeed. Mr. Omarshefsky gave me the paper in which the reporter says, "Madam Russell...."

Sofia, Tuesday, May 23

Jim has had a wonderful time. He has made many friends. Today we lunched with the Prime Minister at a club.

The rooms were not large. The tables were about ten each. Jim was happily placed with Swedish people, the Hogquists, the Dutch and several good Germans. He said he felt friendly with them all and was able to use English and German and Spanish as well as his very good French.

We have just come home from visiting Mr. Peerwitz. We had a nice tea at his house. A charming apartment, the furniture all made by hand in old Bulgarian designs. We were asked about school questions, and it was interesting. Mr. Omarschefsky listening and Mr. Peerwitz translating.

We then dressed in our best bib and tucker and went to the reception this evening. We drove over in a taxi, a big Packard. Driving into the place, which was policed, there was a huge crowd gathered on all sides. Two huge spotlights played on the national flag. White, bright red and clear bright green. The flags were long and hung the length of the building. The students were lined up in a single row from the main door up either side of the staircase all the way to the great hall. They were all in evening clothes or else native costume. Very colorful and smart.

As I went up the stairs and arrived at the landing. A line of girls greeted us.

The gathering was particularly brilliant. Every man was wearing his full decorations and the ladies in their finest.

The King arrived and the choir sang several selections. Then as we all stood talking, we suddenly saw the crowd part and there in a cleared circle, about sixteen feet from us, stood King Boris talking to the Chancellor. In a moment, a French professor was brought up to him and the Chancellor fell back, and the King and the Professor began to talk. The Chancellor then came over to Will and said the King wished to talk to him. We were quite restless as the King and the French Professor talked. Will stood there like the prized ox; calm, dignified and quite at ease chatting with the Chancellor. The messenger then appeared to bring Lord Percy from England and he took his stand behind Will. For some unexplained reason, I felt a sense of pleasure at seeing the English Lord Percy behind Will on the list.

The King and Will had such a vivacious and happy interview that afterwards Mrs. Hogquist said, "you amused him well". It was true for during one little interchange they had the King said, "I've seen you before have I not?" Will said, "Yes, Your Majesty". Then he told when it had been and the King began to smile broadly and said, "Then I was young and had a thick head of hair and you were young and had a thick head or hair. Now how both of us have changed."

Thereupon they both laughed heartily because now are both quite, quite bald.

The King asked Will to give him the speeches he had delivered at the time of the giving of degrees, but in his own handwriting and signed by him. He thanked Will for his services to Bulgaria. Will inquired for the Queen and the little children and reminded him that he had been a bachelor when he had seen him sixteen years previously. He congratulated him on his lovely wife.

We continued to stand on the front lines, so to speak, for a time and then we edged out. The Germans were all presented and gradually the King worked his way around the group and then we all went into supper.

There the student dancers appeared and did native dances with native costumes. It was very picturesque. Native musicians with bagpipes and flutes, all dressed in khaki colored wool suits outlined in black braid with a tail black wool cap, narrow at the top, perched jauntily on one side and a rose stuck in it somewhere. They paraded around the lovely big room followed by the dancers, two by two. The music is weird and the pointed, turned-up toes of the hemp shoes, the tightly bound leggings and the triple beat of their rhythm seemed strange on the parquet. Amidst such worldly scenes I longed to see it all by moonlight or firelight or torchlight in some small village amidst the shepherds and the people of the country.

Sofia, Wednesday May 24, 1939

We began the day going very early to the place in front of the church. There we were interested in the arrangements.

The square is very large and in the center was an open-air Mass. There was erected an altar on a low platform with arches from the four corners, forming a sort or center. Then the same on the four sides so the whole thing forms a cross with each arm forming another. It was painted white and wound in evergreens, making a very nice center. Round the square there were huge standards, wine, red, white and brilliant green flags. Topping them on one an arrowhead, on the next a lion and strung between them forming a huge festoon around the entire square were ropes of evergreens.

We entered the square between groups of handsome young men in white tunics, caps and gloves with black trousers and polished boots. The West Point of Bulgaria.

Next came the girls from the schools, which Will & I had visited a few days ago. They were all in native dress wearing the accordion pleated short overskirt of their family and the embroidered apron. The family buckles, huge rounds of sliver, were fastened to their belts, and around their necks ancient necklaces and ancient bracelets. Over every ear, very very Bulgarian, a rose. There were three or four girls standing before their group bearing large letters outlined with brilliant blue bachelor's buttons. These letters were very hard ones in the alphabet and were to signify once more that St. Cyril and Methodius had invented the alphabet and various schools and...

...groups from the youngest to the oldest were standing drawn up along the street coming into the square and the best places of honor in the square, and the university students on the step of the church, with their teachers in some special costume or distinctive thing.

One group of little boys had a quill in their cap and a silver trumpet shaped like pipes which, as they marched passed, they played in their haunting, sweet strange voice of a sort or pipe organ. It touched the crowd and as they went by not a hand was raised by the Germans or the Italians. They were listened to with respect. To see these mischievous faces marching so well and to hear them play the music I had a dizzy sensation of a spirit so young and so gay passing me by.

I wanted to join the parade and go with them. I suppose those must be the pipes the Pied Piper used. As the children passed the King's stand, they began to shout letting a sound ring out as they passed by, then continuing it as long as possible, it was a prolonged note almost like a chant. No wonder Bulgarians always have good lungs and are recognized as musicians all over the world.

After the march passed of the schools had been going on for an hour or so, I felt the need of rest and we retreated to the hotel to prepare for Mr. Omarschefsky's party in his home.

We went there and found a new apartment house. A servant let us in, a young man with a keen face and the good look of a saint. Mr. Omarchefsky complained about the dancing at the evening event. He said it was for villages where they dance in the fields. It was a thing of nature. He felt that it was not the thing for a ballroom, but we never having seen it otherwise enjoyed it all the same, though I am sure it would have been better in a country setting. We began the meal with a sort or cocktail of Vodka or Vermouth. Will insisted that his was Vodka so there was much joking about our going to see the King and how we must not go in weaving.

Madam Omarschefsky had a lovely luncheon, very interesting and beautifully done. First there were cucumbers in long pieces which we ate with toothpicks. Then excellent figs with a delicious sauce. Then lamb cooked with rice and mushrooms. Then salad or lettuce and tomatoes and a good dressing. Two tarts made the dessert. They were made by Madam, and one was of a cheese. The other was a sweet and very good, made with nuts and honey. They had beautiful strawberries and whipped cream. Our bread was potato bread made also by Madam and much admired. She afterwards sent us a huge, round loaf to the station.

With French to the right of me, English to the left of me, Germans across from me, and Bulgarians everywhere we had the liveliest of times. Mr. ___said he didn't need English to talk to Will or Will Bulgarian to talk to him and it was true.

We all seemed to understand each other and a perfectly wonderful time together. The spirit of good fellowship was so alive and seemed to be a guest with us. As we were leaving the manservant bid us goodbye and bowed us off exactly as if we were old friends of long standing.

Speaking of the hands or the Germans and the Italians - the first day when the King and Queen arrived, the students began to cheer and the band played the national anthem, the audience rose, and the Italians and Germans, all handsome men and fine looking women dressed gorgeously, flinging up the right arm they went into the Nazi and Fascist salute. It was a feeling of shock. I noticed afterwards entirely before I became used to it, it was amusing to see and more amusing as the moments passed.

The King finally came into the room and then after the close of the national anthem the band went on immediately to the King's hymn. A very dignified professor let his arm fall only to shoot it right up again into its place. So, if the countries outside of the Axis have nothing else at least they could stand and keep and look quite content while those others remained at attention with their hand extended for another fifteen minutes.

At the first meeting I was much struck by the ridiculous sight, but after we had attended the big functions for five days and time after time the same thing happened knowing no German or Italian would dare to let his arm down or fail in his salute as he guarded his life and the welfare of his family, we began to feel sorry for them.

Sofia, Thursday May 25, 1939

Today we had a luncheon for the Omarchefskys at the hotel. Then we went to the station. There we were met by a delegation of people who had studied at Columbia. Mr. Omarchefsky called me and said a band of children were coming to play for us. They came. The brass band played, and the girls formed in a row in front wearing native dress. Then in came the tiny children with their teacher, each one with a bouquet for me or my husband. Some gave them to me, and some gave them to him. Some gave them to Jim. We were so showered with flowers, we soon stood loaded down.

Will was in tears and most of the crowd also. Each little boy or girl made me a little speech saying, these flowers were from the little children of Bulgaria to the little children in America. I thanked them for the little children in America and gave their greetings. They too replied by saying again the little children in Bulgaria greet the little children in America. The band was playing again, and the children all kneeled down, and we discovered that people were weeping. I found it rather hard to keep my end up and at that time I decided that Will should speak to the children, so I asked Miss Cassanova what the way was to say, "thank you" and "goodbye." She said it and one of the Bulgarian ladies said, "Say thank you, dear children." So we called Will and he learned the words.

Then he roared them out for the little children. They gave a surprised and delighted shout, and the band began to play once more, so we went on to the train followed by several of our friends. There were touching farewells and then with our flowers banked in the window we leaned out waving our handkerchiefs and as the band played, we rolled out of the station. I turned around and saw Will standing leaning against the door, his arms full of flowers laughing weakly. He said, "Every day since I've been here my blood pressure gets up to about 400 all at once." The last word was had by our friend Mr. Black who came over to the window and quietly delivered Mrs. Black's last message, saying: "Mrs. Black says, "The Germans will be green all the way to Berlin". The 89 representing Germany are not all on this train. We have about 10 of them, and quite a number of Italians

Now we are traveling again through Yugoslavia. One of the passengers is a German gentleman, a very tall, handsome, distinguished looking man wearing the finest clothes of the best quality and traveling with his manservant. They have the first-class cabin next to mine. They sent word that he was leaving for the next car to be with his lady friend and that we could have our connecting door open and use his cabin. So now we're settled down with flowers in the basins in the corner. We pushed up the top and it stands against the window making a nice dark mahogany background for the enormous flowers all lovely white, pink and American beauty peonies with long stems, marguerites, roses, Iris, bachelors buttons, pampas grass. It all looks very beautiful to see them up against the countryside.

Editor's Note: Chloe & Will later returned to the USA on the Ile de France. Only three months later, on the eve of WWII, she was the last civilian ship to leave France. During the war, she was stripped of her luxurious fittings and served carrying materiel, troops and POWs[1].

[1] SS Ile de France, in Wikipedia. https://en.wikipedia.org/wiki/SS_%C3%8Ele_de_France

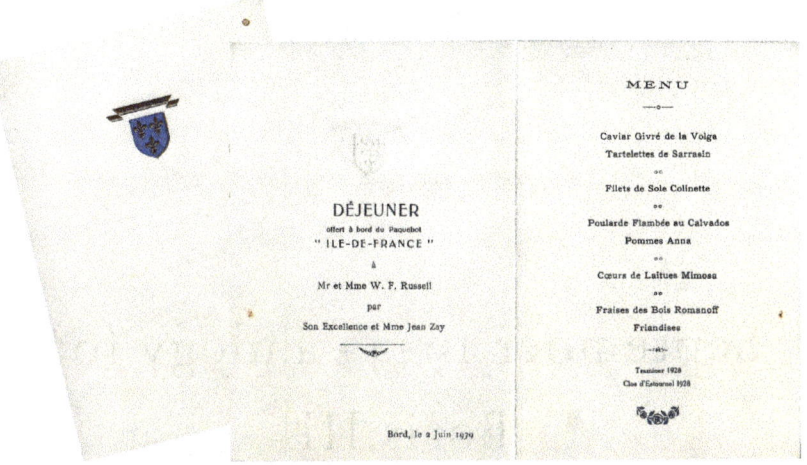

Personalized menu from the return voyage on the Ile de France
Russell Family Archives

7

September 1943 - Eulogy for Boris III

Editor's Introduction: Boris III of Bulgaria died on August 28, 1943, following a meeting with Hitler in which Boris III refused to deport Bulgarian Jews to concentration camps or to join Germany on its Eastern Front against Russia. Shortly thereafter he died a heart attack, although theories exist that he was poisoned. Dismayed by the sudden death of the kind and modest monarch she had just met, Chloe wrote this eulogy.

The Day I Saw it Plain

The scene is Sofia. The date is May 18, 1939. The place is the square which spreads out like an amphitheater before the main building of the University of Bulgaria

The yellow bricks paving the square are hot. The sun beats down on us and blazes off the golden miters of six bearded Bishops. They intone the Greek Mass, at an altar erected in the open air. This is a very special occasion, the celebration of the 50th anniversary of the founding of the modern University of Bulgaria.

A large crowd is gathered close to the center reserved for the religious observance. We come from many nations, invited to assist at the anniversary celebration. Our group of six or seven Americans stands together. We watch and listen.

Drawn up in formation along the outer rim of the square are the school children and their teachers. Each school is represented by a selected group. The girls wear proudly the silver jewelry which has come down to them in their families for generations. It is set off by their colorfully embroidered aprons, and sheer, white, full-sleeved blouses. They have roses in their hair — Bulgarian roses. They chat and laugh — pretty, modern girls!

The young boys wear tunic blouses with the upstanding collars of colored embroidery buttoned to one side, and peaked caps. The colors of the caps denote the wearer's section or stage in school. Serene, healthy, happy youth of a nation where youth goes unthwarted and unexploited. Suddenly, an unostentatious open car is driven into the square. The King and Queen!

He wears a white uniform with tunic and cap displaying gold insignia. The Queen is charming in a gray chapeau and mink jacket. They sail gaily around the square in front of the lines of children who begin to cheer. One after another, young voices take up the sound. A continuous note rises and falls, from group to group, for all the world like a football cheer in a round. Not a spontaneous cheer, but a sincere one — and beautiful!

The perfect accompaniment of the arrival of a Balkan King!

Some of us think of Graustark, but I think of the Greek chorus. Perhaps this is all we have of the popular customs of Ancient Greece. Their music vanished for want of a written symbol; even their Democracy vanished. Could our beautiful music also vanish? Could our children forget forever? Can these beautiful children fall into the hands of those who will tear from them their priceless heritage - their traditions? I find such troubling thoughts crossing my mind.

The car comes to a stop. The Sovereigns descend. The Bishops can be heard intoning the Mass. We watch as the celebration comes to an end and a sequence of interviews begins, between the King, the Queen, the guests, and the different groups of children. The teachers are to be seen in earnest conversation as they present their charges. The children are keenly aware. They are silent, watchful and proud. We, mere spectators, wander out of the square and pass down the gay, crowded street. A parade is to be the next event. Some rows of seats have been erected along the front of the clubhouse opposite to the park.

One of our friends is there saving some places for us. He is in bad humor and grumbles about German servants saving all the seats in the front row for their masters. I begin to reason with him, "Why do they want the front row? One can see much better from this third row", said I. "Right," said he, "But from the front row one can be much better seen! I heard them giving the instructions to the servants to save their places. That is why I hurried here. This occasion is to be used to convince the people of something — take it from me; the Germans never do anything for nothing."

The parade begins. The children are passing. They are smiling gaily — all eyes toward our stands. Now I begin to see what my friend was grumbling about. From their places along the curb opposite the stands, the parents can see just one long line of Germans. They are just the right number to fill the front two rows. Sweat pours off their heads; in their heavy academic robes they look warm and foolish. Each and every one with right hand stretched stiff in the Nazi salute. Their wives and the obliging servants, all very richly garbed, all saluting as if their lives depended on it. The scarlet velvet robes encrusted with scrolls of gold galloon — with a red and gold biretta, representing German academia. The dark green velvet with the mink cape and tricorne cap; the robes of the law school with bibs of white pleated linen — and all the fine display of traditional splendor and symbolic learning.

We sit for a while, dodging, trying to see something of the parade through the forest of Nazi hands. Then we decide to give up our places to some of the Bulgarians, who continue to smile with delight as they crane their heads and dodge, hoping for a glimpse of their own special pride and joy.

The procession is passing swiftly as we reach a quiet spot. The children seem to be drawn down the broad avenue as if by enchantment.

I begin to feel breathless. What do the Bulgarian people have, that these Nazis want? Why have ninety ugly rogues come with their wives, calling themselves Professors, sporting minks and sables? And since when did Professors' salaries warrant such a display of diamonds and sables? Why are they here, bringing a gift of ten thousand volumes for the University Library? Eleven thousand dollars in gold, and many other valuable gifts?

Why these signs of devotion to Bulgaria and the Bulgarians? Why are they attending the 50th anniversary celebration of the University of Sofia?

There are nine Frenchmen, old, fat, full of years, good humor and simplicity, and no ceremony at all. There are six Englishmen, as quiet and unostentatious as the French savants, though somewhat more ceremonious. A dignified Norwegian couple: the gentle and beautiful wife and modest husband so exactly what we would expect a distinguished scholar to be. The Poles, the Hungarians, the Hollanders, the Belgians, indeed, representatives of all the countries all looking and behaving as our customs have taught us they should.

Contrasted to these, this tawdry band of nervous Germans seems to be sweeping the entire affair, like witches on a broom. Everything is losing its meaning. All the dear little things and people; the roses in the hair of the girls; those silver pipes played upon so gaily by the band of boys; the beautifully executed folk dances, so swiftly performed by the youths in their straw sandals, snowy wool trousers and high embroidered hats. They are being rudely pushed aside; they execute their leaps, and shout and turn, but we go on thinking of the Germans.

Suddenly we know it. A chill wind seems to be blowing over us. We look at one another. As we turn again, we study them, to watch the strange marionettes — hands still stretched up in the Nazi salute — their tiring arms need to be jerked to attention. They shine with still more sweat. A rush of comprehension sweeps over us; this is the enemy:

here in our midst. No guns! Just gifts, smiles and money! Poor Bulgaria! Poor, dear, charming children - may God help you and keep you.

With this prayer in our hearts, that bright day vanishes from our mind's eye, and we are back again in 1943.

There is an old Bulgarian custom — when they like you, they ask you to share their ceremonial bread. You are asked to dip a morsel of the bread in some salt. Then, when you have eaten it, you become one of them. Some days after the scene I have described above, we were gathered together at the Sofia railroad station. A group of Bulgarian friends had given us a jolly party, and were seeing us off with music and flowers, and many gifts.

Amongst the gifts we were given a large warm loaf of their broad; the women who gave it to me said, "Here, when you eat some of it, think of us. We want you to be one of us. We did not know you when you came, so we could not ask you. Now you are leaving. Before you cross the border, dip a morsel in some salt and become a Bulgarian!"

I thanked her and made room in my arms for the precious loaf, passing a few of my flowers to my son. Our party was beginning to wear the air of a true and lasting God-Speed. Our friends had brought generous bouquets from their superb gardens. My husband, son, and I were all loaded down with flowers. The children accompanying their parents, wearing their native dress in our honor.

The boys' group was one of the school bands. One group of little girls sang songs for us. A tiny child detached herself from the group and ran up to me to give me her present. It was a wee bouquet of forget-me-nots arranged with a few yellow rose buds.

We were delighted and anxious to thank the children personally. I had an inspiration and asked young woman: "How does one say, 'Thank you, dear little children' in Bulgarian?" She told me, and I asked her to demonstrate it to my husband. At first, he looked amazed; then, looking at the little group drawn up so properly and back at me. He saw me pleading with him, over my flowers and my loaf of precious bread; he gazed then at his own arms, filled with blossoms, realizing this was no mere au revoir, but we must wish them farewell.

So he walked toward the children who became silent. To the surprise of everyone, the words he said were Bulgarian. "Dear Friends, Farewell, Adieu, Adieu!" As they recognized their own tongue, a delighted shout arose. The train came in. The bend played, and we were off, waving our handkerchiefs, on our way to Belgrade.

In our stateroom we found ourselves surrounded with all those flowers. I clutched my bread, with tears streaming down my face. I began to explain that I must be a Bulgarian already. Then I realized that my husband was mopping his eyes also.

Suddenly we heard a knock at the door. A tall, good-looking man entered. He spoke English with an accent and introduced himself as a Hollander, who often travelled through Bulgaria. He was smiling and said: "I am sure you will be amused. Those Germans who boarded the train in Sofia, were so mad about the send-off the people were giving you Americans, that they were cursing, and all pulled down the window shades. I've never been so happy in my life."

We gave him some roses and shook his hand. We had met our first messenger from the haunts of free men. He rejoiced to see clear-cut evidence of the place the Bulgarians wanted to be. They, as well as ourselves, were on the right side, and sides had already been drawn. He went out saying: "Those Nazis will be mad all the way to Berlin."

Needless to say, we ate the bread, and we believe we have a bond of sympathy with all that is Bulgarian.

The vise they are held in is of no moments forging. The thoroughness of the job is attested to by the fact that a German firm years ago, with no possible hope of a good financial gain, built in far-off Sofia, a large modern hotel. Another company put in an excellent water system. An electric power plant was built, all with German funds the people were glad to benefit. Then, one day, they awoke to the fact that anyone disagreeing with all those so-called improvements, was likely to have an interview with a hard-eyed person who recalled that it was wise to know what side one's bread was buttered on. The army was small and headed by only men trained in Germany. They were the only ones owning arms. The Germans had a determined hold on Bulgaria ten years ago! The people watched uneasily.

The King came in for some of the blame. However, our friends seemed genuinely fond of Boris. When I praised the lovely floral decorations in the Palace or on the tables of the various functions, I was told, with apparent pride, that the King was responsible for the quality of the flowers and fruit. Any rulers would have enemies. Boris' enemies were not amongst the Bulgarian people. They seemed to feel genuine affection for him. Some intellectuals and the politicians were indeed his deadly enemies. The people were frightened, and they could not distinguish their friends amongst some of their own people. They were on guard, but helpless. So, also, was their King.

So now they are obliged to assist as spectators, or — worse — as collaborators in a fight they would love to have helped to wage on the side of right — not might. Their position is all the more painful since, to them, Russia is holy. They speak of "Holy Russia" "Mother Russia", "Little Russia" Russians are their brothers.

Saint George is the patron saint of Bulgaria. In the shops, where the handicrafts were on display, one could always see many beautiful silver images of him. The artists usually depicted him killing the dragon. I was told there is an old legend that the dragon was slain by St. George in Bulgaria. Legend tells that the dragon was heavily covered with armor, from his nostrils came stream of liquid fire. Not a tank — not a flame-thrower, but the dragon's terror ended in Bulgaria.

Boris, like other helpless people, had no choice. His army was dominated by Germans. His commerce was in their hands. He stood between the people and the Nazis. Hence, he perished, though protected by his people and safe amongst them. Hitler had called him to a conference. A striking parallel exists between that conference and one Napoleon held at a similar time in history.

Napoleon, driven from Russia, was on his way back to France. He paused for a few days in Dresden. Deciding he must have fresh troops, he sent for King Francis II from Vienna. The King did not go himself but he sent the ablest man in Austria - the man who knew France and the French language to perfection, Count Metternich — a man of the noblest heritage — and the finest product of the culture of his day. Napoleon was walking up and down in a black mood, when Metternich arrived. No interpreter was needed. The interview took place in private and lasted eight hours.

Napoleon demanded the entrance of the Austrians (heretofor neutral) into the war. He had his officers training an Austrian army of 300,000 men. Now he called for them from his new father-in-law! However, the interview has no witnesses - and no report was made. As Metternich left the conference he was questioned for news. His reply was: "The Emperor has given me all the light I desire." He was permitted to return to Austria, where Napoleon expected him to convince the King that he should order the Army to advance on the Russians, bringing in the required number of men and the supplies to stop the rout of the French army.

Metternich worked like one possessed. He arranged a treaty with Czar Nicholas — agreeing to bring up the Austrian forces to aid the Russians. Then he informed Napoleon of this treaty and gave him an ultimatum. "An armistice, or we march with the Russians!" Napoleon was silent until the time of the ultimatum had expired, Then, when he saw nothing else to do, he granted the armistice which was in reality a capitulation.

Hitler, they say, has studied Napoleon's history and has modeled his own mad career on that of the world conquerors who have gone before him. Napoleon was vain, so Hitler dresses humbly. Napoleon enjoyed the company of beautiful women. So, to avoid what Hitler felt were the pitfalls which ruined Napoleon, he has been quite untouched by feminine wiles. Could it be that seeing himself in the same boat with Napoleon — defeated and driven from Russia, — he turned to his history and as he called upon the army of 300,000 men his generals had assembled and trained in Bulgaria, — he vowed not to fall into the pitfall into which Napoleon sank. So — no emissary would do for him — the King must come. If he did not agree to Hitler's terms, he must be removed. For, if Boris had lifted his voice and called for Bulgarians to join their Russian brothers — he could have become as powerful as Metternich. Instead, he is gone.

Coming events cast their shadows before, and what seemed insignificant in the bright light of the noon, when France fell and London shook under the blitzkrieg, may loom great across the land as the sun of Nazidom sets. A small force may once more turn the tide.

Goethe said of Metternich: "He is one of those men who inspires the consoling assurance that reason and humanity will triumph, and that clear intelligence will soon rule over this chaotic situation in which we are living." Metternich, writing to his daughter, said: "I must appear to Napoleon as a sort of conscience personified. I have told and re-told it all to him in Dresden. The evils have now been stopped by the decree of heaven."

We have lost the man most able to act as conscience to Hitler - the man most able to speak for all of us.

Boris was half-French. He knew the language and spoke it to perfection. He knew and loved England and the English - spoke graceful English, with but a slight accent. He was fine mechanic and said — if relieved of his duties as an executive, he wanted to come to the United States and gain his living as an expert mechanic. He performed his duties perfectly and as I write; it hurts me to remember him; and the realization that the ugly and the hateful triumphed, is painful.

Hitler was too smart to follow Napoleon into that pitfall, but God is not mocked. Perhaps, in little Bulgaria a shadow begins to grow larger.

Can we make up for wasted opportunity? Can we help the Bulgarians to join us in fact, — as they have long ago, in spirit?

Boris III of Bulgaria
Photo Credit: https://kingsimeon.bg

8

Some Spies I Have Known

Chloe & Will traveled to Venice in the late autumn of 1953
Russell Family Archives

Editors Introduction: It seems probable that this brief essay was an assignment from Chloe's later studies in creative writing. I include it here because the man described - named as "Mr. Ziegler" - makes an appearance in Chloe's travelogue from 1946, having used the information he gathered against the French. The delicious irony of this essay is that the spy Chloe knew best was in fact her husband, as WFR was involved in intelligence activity for the US from 1918, only a few years after they married.

Spy is a word that for some reason, possibly Mata Hari, has been surrounded with clouds of fantasy.

There was a very tall, elegant, and mysterious French woman who came to this country trailing clouds of glamor. Her name was Gaby Deslys. I thought she must be a spy. She looked like my idea of a spy. But that was long ago.

So, when the day came for me to meet a real Spy, I did not recognize him. He was a German who had married a French woman and spoke several languages fluently and almost perfect English. He had good manners and went with us for the expeditions in the high mountains of the Pyranees. I used to particularly enjoy his company for I enjoy German poetry well spoken. I told him and he would be quoting away, Der Erl Koenig, or some other beautiful piece, as we climbed.

The French dancer Gaby Deslys
Russell Family Archives

This annoyed my husband, who grew up in Germany and loved passionately what he called, "Dear, delightful, disorderly France." So naturally it spoiled the joy in his mind's eye of the water-falls and sweeps of beauty to hear rumbling away behind him, "Wer reitet so spaet durch Nacht und Wind?"

So finally, my husband said that it irked him, and the poetry sessions ended, but the man continued to haunt all of our trips.

Later the German wrote to my husband and asked for some more detailed descriptions of a special place. My husband did not answer and shortly France fell. After the war, we received the news that the delightful quoter of poetry had returned to the mountains in uniform and in charge of troops. He personally directed the search of caves and the destruction of paths, so that no one could hide or even escape through those parts of the high mountains.

Now when I think of a Spy, I can see a clean-cut, blue-eyed man wearing a French beret, a Scotch tweed jacket and baggy golf trousers with his mountain boots. He has good manners and quotes poetry.

9

The Contrabandier

Editor's Note: The following is most likely another creative writing assignment and preserves Chloe's deep affection for the people and culture of the Pyrenees.

Does the word shepherd bring up a picture in your mind's eye? Do you think of a man clad in a long, flowing robe, wearing a turban and holding a crook in his hand?

I had an experience with shepherds, and it was such a vivid and picturesque one that it stayed with me

To begin with, we were doing some long walks on the French side of the Pyrenees mountains. There they have a special breed of mountain sheep with horns coiled besides their heads. They are so beautiful they make one thing of stone sculptures. Of course, they do, because when an artist has wanted to carve a sheep, he chooses to show them in their rhythmic, sphinx-like beauty.

These sheep have wool of special softness and fineness so that the French woolens are particularly valued for women's garments.

The flocks go up into the high mountains in early summer and stay there grazing until fall, so one sees large numbers of those sheep and always the man and his dog tending them.

The Basque shepherds are dark and rough-voiced and clad in black. Most often they wear black corduroy trousers and around the waist is wound, smooth and tight, a sort of scarf. It is called a ceinture and is about three yards long. It is finely woven by hand and is a very useful thing for anyone in the mountains. It serves to pull up things and people or to let them down cliffs or rough places. It is necessary equipment and takes up little room.

They wear a black beret pulled well forward over one eye and have a jacket of khaki colored wool. It is often worn toga-line on one shoulder. For bad weather, they wear a great, long, black wool cape. Their boots are the heavy-soled mountain boots with iron spikes, but usually they wear their canvas-rope soled espadrilles.

They sing a song – nothing like "Bring me my boots and my saddle."

It goes, "O mon beret, o mon beret – give me my espadrilles and my beret!"

So if you can imagine a neat, soft-stepping modest sort of man, smelling strongly of tobacco, whose manners are most formal and courteous; whose voice is rough and low; whose eyes are very black and humorous; all garbed in black with a small, active little dog of a sparse sort of shagginess, there you can imagine a Basque Shepherd.

We had often seen them and spoken to them in their lonely vigil, high on some mountain. Then one night after a long climb through a storm that rained "pitchforks," we arrived at the little stone mountain Refuge.

We opened the door and inside all was bright. The room was filled with smoke and a bright fire was blazing in the crude, stone fireplace. Along the walls, seated on the stone benches were several of the shepherds. They turned black eyes toward us and deep voices greeted us. Their little dogs were crouched at their feet.

I wanted so much to sit down and listen to their talk, but I knew my place as a woman and a stranger, so went on into the next room reserved for serving coffee, for such as we.

When they began to leave, one after another they rose, knocked out the pipe in the fireplace, and taking the dog under one arm, they bade us good night and went out into the storm to care for their flocks.

Their little dogs are used to being carried if it storms or if they have to climb. The dogs cannot climb, but cling to the shoulders of their masters. They understand every word and run to execute military-like deployments of the sheep.

While we were in the inner room drinking coffee a man came in and spoke to me. He said he was Spanish, and his eyes were blue as the sea. He told me that he knew me I was quite surprised until he had explained where he had met me in Spain, and he was quite right.

He brought out a bottle of brandy to drink a toast with us. It was something special, he said. Inside the bottle there were several pale golden straws and clustered along the straws were crystals.

The owner of the refuge – the Patron – explained to us that they were sugar crystals and that this was something very fine. The Spaniard was bringing it across the border quite against the law, so he was called the "Contrabandier." I exclaimed that it must be dangerous to be called so. He and the others laughed,

"We call everyone names like that," they explained, "Guide we call Guide; Climber we call Montagnard, etc."

I who almost never taste alcohol drank the toast he proposed for us, and we returned his good wishes. Before he left, he asked,

"You like this brandy, Madam?" I said, "Yes indeed." Then he said grandly, "Very well, I will bring you a bottle."

He did do so and the next time we came to the Refuge, I received my gift. I carried it carefully under my arm, all the way home to New York and that winter we toasted the French sitting behind their useless Maginot line! We did so hope and pray that their day of trial would not come.

The end of the story?

We went back after the War. We climbed up to the Refuge and there were no sheep in sight and the beautiful white cows were all gone, but the Refuge was there and the Patron was there trying to open it up for the summer.

It was a sad reunion. We asked about the Shepherds. They were doing fairly well. What about the Contrabandier?

Too.... Too bad. They caught him and shot him.

I said a Deo Gratias for the shepherds and then I said Requiescat in Pace for the Contrabandier.

10

April 1946 - Sailing on the Ile de France

Postcard from Russell Family Archives

Editor's Introduction: For this second travelogue, I have included not only Chloe's notes, but also her letters home to her son, Bob (in italics). These include incremental observations and deepen the experience of travel with her. Chloe & Will were among the first to return to Europe aboard their beloved

Ile de France. Stripped of her luxury and still serving as a troopship, it would be another year before the ship was restored to her former luxury state.

Boston, April 26, 1946

Arrived and Elise and I took a taxi to the Somerset. There we were given a newly furnished suite. Everything is cold and rainy. Soon a call came and a box of orchids from Mercy Hayes. Then another call and in came Libby and Bobby. He had tears in his eyes because he had missed meeting us at the train. However, we decided to go right out to see Tory and Erland and Bob and to stay for supper. So, we began to feel gay and had no more signs of tears.

Tory met us at the door looking beautiful and also looking for "Bahpa" who was coming next day. We all went up to see Elise's room. The playroom fixed over just for her. Very comfortable. Then we had supper in the candlelight, and I went home early so Bob could study.

April 27, 1946

The next day I got up early, went to town with Elise and I had a headache so back to bed. Will came about four o'clock and he and Elise went out to Bob's and they all had dinner at Lochobers.

Saturday it was raining. We took little Tory and Bobby and went to Sears for some new shoes. Good luck. When we passed through the narrow way leading in from Winter Street, Libby said "I couldn't make it through here six weeks ago." In buying shoes we were waited on by a young man just out of service, He took an x-ray and we saw the little bones lying exactly right. Then we had lunch at the hotel and shopped for some books and out to the pier to get our luggage put on the ship. Back to the hotel and all in order by 5 p.m. and once more dinner in the hotel.

The books we got were Top Secret, Eisenhower, The Ballad, The Source, Dickens, Works of Plato, Charlotte and Emily Bronte, and One World or None. Bob and Libby each were wearing gardenias, and I had my orchids, so we looked as if we were ready for a farewell party. It's nice to see Bob and Libby waltz. It seemed a reminder of an era that began with the Waltz and ended with the same.

Bob drove us down to the boat, the Ile de France, coming as far as the barrier where they left us. We were called up as American citizens, given a little boost and then we went on board.

We were met at the gangplank by our waiter-to-be with the gentle French touch right off. He guided us to our room. As he passed along the plain white corridors with grey cement underfoot and pipes overhead, he would show us where bits of the old ship still were intact, spaces of wrought iron railings, the chapel, some of the stairs and so forth. It was sad to see the completeness of the change from a luxury liner to a troop ship.

This was the first passage of the Ile de France after the war as a ship carrying a few passengers. I could not help feeling happy about it all. It seemed to say that the French people had not drawn back at any sacrifice.

At last, I could feel the completeness of war-effort I had associated this only with the English. The ship pleased me as it is. I'm glad to sleep in a bunk with a hard mattress. We have good white wool blankets and good French sheets. Every necessary comfort, but none of the luxurious excess of former times. It seems good somehow.

Each day we must all report for breakfast before nine.

7:30 is Mass and then the mess. Lunch is at 11:30 for children and 12:30 for adults and then we have dinner at 7:30 and the children at 6:30. The dining room is laid out with mostly long white tables with eight at each. There are bowls of flowers for each table and white tablecloths. Coffee is poured out of big, brown, earthenware pots which keep hot and then hot milk is served. The meals are good. All in all, we have everything we need and always the best of service.

So far it has been sleep for most all day. Yesterday we had a lunch with the Captain with cocktails first in his cabin. We met some jolly people. Later we had tea in the Colonel's room and we also met some pleasant people there. A good time in both places. Movies each afternoon. At last, I got to the canteen to buy a notepad. We were taken on a tour of inspection of the installations for the troops, they are astounding.

Today we were on deck and enjoyed seeing the painting operations beginning once more. This ship will no doubt again become one of the best.

Lunch with the Captain was just as before the war. Today we had a casserole for lunch. I almost wept into it. I should have if I didn't for the waiter said it was the first since the war.

April 29, 1946

We went to 7:30 Mass this morning and then breakfast of bacon and shirred eggs and Will and I took a walk. The sea is calm, but a cool breeze blowing and more wind coming. We went to the lounge where the little English doctor came in with ___ the Russian writer and pianist. We had a nice time chatting and he told about living in a castle near Berchtesgaden.

He is doing an article for the Saturday Evening Post. A film after lunch "The Corn is Green." Tea with the young Mabilles.

Tuesday, April 30, 1946
"Dear Bob,
We got off to a good start. I can't begin to tell you of all the changes on the ship. You would feel that there had never been any of the lovely decorations, except for the chapel. That is untouched. We go there to Mass every morning and try to remember all the handsome things gone forever.

The food is so good (today Cassoulet! Beans & meat!). It's quite a thrill to see what can be done with the right cook to do it. We are all in the tourist dining room. Everything is one big Army transport. All the ceiling panels, etc. pulled out — they are to take 9,000 men going back!

Don't forget to jog Elise's memory to go to the Boston Guild for the Hard of Hearing on the 17th. It is in the telephone book. She must take the best and most comfortable and most suitable device. I hope she can find a good one. She is due to go the 17th. Send the bill for the device home to Miss Sheridan c/o Teacher's College. Make sure, won't you?

We had lunch with the Captain and tea with the Canadian Colonel the first day out. Lots of fun.

Yesterday, a Dr. Mabille came, and we all had tea. Today our visit was with Seraff – a pianist – he is reporting on to the Prague and Salzburg music festivals and he was so interesting. He told about living in an old Chateau in the hills near Berchtesgaden, seeing Hitler, etc. While living there one day an English girl walked in on leave – the story is a good one – he used a bicycle all the time in the old palace, it was so big he rode from room to room! He is funny and no doubt very clever. He is writing an article on the ship.

We also saw the film "The Corn is Green" – very good. Had tea with two charming French young people – what they tell about things is as raw as can be!

Well, inform Miss Sheridan of the cost of the ear contrivance and make sure Elise gets it. Give my love to all my darlings,

We are having a really good time.

Love Mother"

Thursday May 2, 1946.

Went to bed too late last night and missed Mass this morning. Then up to the lounge where I talked to Anne Colby Vanderbilt. She told about Curacao, how the ships came in there all on fire and sinking. The boys were rescued from the burning oil, and some were saved but many died. She helped by speaking English with the ones who could speak English. When the ARROW was torpedoed, the Captain steered her into the harbor one half in a huge blaze. The boys were jumping off into the sea of blazing oil. The priests and a Major in the Army put out in a motorboat and cruised about until they had rescued all they could. Many died later from their burns.

The authorities ordered the Captain out to sea. He steered the ship on out and then beached her far at the end of the island. The firefighters went out there and put out the fire and removed the bombs and the depth charges etc. The ship was half gutted.

The Captain was decorated for keeping her afloat. However, when they moved her for the renovations she sank and was lost in the end.

Other such tales kept me listening for three hours.

After lunch and tea, we have seen the Mabilles and are on the way to dinner with the Captain. The poor steward said to me in answering my question about how to dress, said "C'est le diner du Commandant!" So it's to be gayer this evening. I put on my only formal dress, but as I went down the steps, I noticed that no one else was wearing a long dress so I went back and took it off so I would not do differently from the others. I had the place of honor at the right of the Commander. Across from me sat General Simmons who was an aide to Montgomery.

He told interesting things about his campaign such as the saying that radar and the Bailey bridge and the jeeps and the landing craft had won the war. But no one let him talk. Each woman to the right and left of him kept him pinned down. One with a high voice lecturing him on what Canada should do about educating its children, and the other side a Mrs. Jones, gentle and determined, told him all about what she did during the war.

She worked in a canteen where many sailors passed through.

One man would say "How's about it, sister? How's about a Coke for a bloke?" She said that he came two or three times and always demanded "a Coke for a bloke." She saw him recently returning after three years. She went up to him and said, "I suppose you want a Coke for a bloke." And he cried, "You remember me!"

The General would get in a word now and then but not many. I wish I could have heard more. He told of having the staff from the flag that flew from the front of Rommel's car. Someone else has the flag but he has the staff. Also, as they passed through all the campaign flags were made and finally in Bremen, I think it was, they were all hung over Monty's headquarters. He was given the whole string as a gift.

Also, Churchill would send messages to Monty, and he received personal notes before and after each big engagement. Monty has preserved them all and General Simmons has a replica that he had made. It is very interesting. I would like to see it.

On my left was a Frenchman who was in Japan all through the war. He lost thirty pounds. He is very frail looking but so happy. He and his wife and daughter were well-dressed with clothing bought in New York, quite lovely looking. All very religious. Each morning they were at mass and taking communion.

The Captain is very good altogether. The dinner was excellent. The French chef had taken the army food and done it up in dream fashion. Turkey in thin, thin slices and our plates fixed for us like little works of art and tasting divine.

The dessert was ice cream made on the ship and little wafers. It was nearly impossible to think of it as army fare.

We toasted France, the Captain, happy days and so forth.

Dinner over we were supposed to go to the lounge for an entertainment. I was very tired and wanted to go straight to bed but when I saw the poor French in the lounge, pale with chagrin saying they had saved places for us all by "Force majeur." I felt sorry for those poor men. I could see how it was on them to look at the elegant old ship which had been decorated with such perfection in the old days, when the Captain's dinner was such a social affair and an important thing in their lives.

I realized it was the first Captain's dinner on the French liner after the war and they were trying to have it given great consideration, but it was brushed off quite brusquely. The English went off smartly to bed. I said to Will, "We can't just go to bed." So, we two alone went in and settled ourselves to be entertained.

Soon an American lady, Mrs. McJannette, a very nice person, came. A few moments later the Frenchman from Japan came so we had five mustered out of 18. We felt better for the poor steward who had expected so bright an evening. I had a feeling we were to be given a glimpse of something such as I had seen before the war. I could see that the English didn't deserve to be given the top spot. The way I feel now after seeing the General and his wife and all of them turn their backs and walk off with no feeling of polite duty to their host.

Honestly it is too much like before the war. I was shocked as if I were with Germans. Can it be that they have not learned that when they take privileges from someone else, something is due? Not money, of course, but they must sacrifice their comfort. They accepted the compliment of the dinner but when it came to doing honor to the poor cooks and the stewards they declined and went to bed. Also, another English woman, the daughter of a General Gordon. She's six feet tall and when she goes to the movies each day, she carries her lifejacket and sits on it, giving her a four-inch advantage over everyone else. I did not know what went on in the poor French heads but my neighbor the American lady, resolved to tell the world "I will give a blast."

11

May 1946 - Paris

Editor's Introduction: The "Big Four" conference referred to below was part of the negotiations among the heads of state and foreign ministers of the victorious nations following WWII. The Paris 1946 negotiations were contentious and ended in ill will[1]

"Claridge Hotel, May le _ 1946
Dear Bob,
We had a perfect time coming over. Sea like a lake the whole way. At Cherbourg we had to get up at 5am and the wind was howling and very cold. At 9:15 we stepped on the tender and came up to the dock. The sight was just wonderful.

The docks – the old sights all ravished completely, but in place of the old things the submarine pens – still there – 3 – out by the big breakwater. A hole had been smashed in 2 or 3 places but replaced. The big old structures for the piers are still all boarded up and badly bombed out – however we landed and were welcomed by the Chef of the Commercial Club (Chamber of Commerce), the Mayor, Head of the French Line, etc., etc.! It was fun. They insisted on sending us into town for a lunch at a hotel. The French Line had given us box lunches, but we went to town in their car – with the young man who is the engineer of the new constructions.

It was awfully nice – the old town exactly as before – nothing touched but the people. They are gay and chattering and they go and come in hordes. However, they look very hard put to it – their skins are all broken out, their poor legs purple with cold and NO stockings at all. Mostly the children have socks, but the women all go bare-legged. It was so bitter and cold I was sorry for them.

Their shoes were all done up with wooden soles. They are very pretty, but they do not look too easy to walk with. They have open toes, stacked heels and straps around the ankles. The finest shoes at home are designed just this way, but we use leather. The soles here all seem to be of wood – even of the men's shoes.

The meal was delicious. We had dried pea soup first, then poached sole. It tasted fine to us, but I think the French would all have liked some meat. The vegetable was cauliflower, very good. Then dessert was one of those custards that come in an envelope. Tasted fine. Then a piece of cheese and with it all black bread. Then the Café National, that is charred chestnuts. I liked it, but the French made a face and said "well, it is hot."

Dad insisted on paying for all four of us. It cost $15 – so you can see it was dear, but we didn't want to charge it to the French Line or our hosts. Our hosts however, then took us to dinner on the train down to Paris.

We had a great time watching the signs of battles – we know nearly every foot of the way. To see the big German tanks all rusting out in the fields, the remains of French locomotives broken into pieces and piled up in a field and all the wreckage of the gigantic battles that tore the place to pieces – to see them all in neat piles gathered in one pasture or place – made you realize that the French are ready to work hard. They want to clear away the scars and begin again. I felt such admiration for those neat old country people. They make France French again already.

It was touching to see the numbers of new roofs and the convents and churches turned out. At Caen we saw real devastation. What a frightful battle raged right there! No doubt about it, that's where the Germans gave all they had. Poor old Monty. He had the big name, so the Germans feared us the less. The whole peninsula, Cherbourg particularly, shows where the main fight raged – it was at Caen. There are miles of that city as flat as your hand. Of course, there is also a lot still standing - the cathedral is right there!

At Lisieux too – the drive to St. Therese (the little flower) is still there. It was badly damaged but is already in a good state of repair.

Well – the lovely apple trees were all in bloom in Normandy. There were cows in the fields, queer thin looking ones, but cows, nevertheless. The trees were there, some scorched by gun fire, but trees and still green, still going strong.

The hedges were still there – the shell holes and so on are not gone yet – we even saw a big American bomber lying in a swamp. However, it is being rapidly done up and will soon be restored to La Belle France.

When we arrived here, we checked our luggage and came here with just one tiny bag by Metro. It was quite and dark and very few cars.

Sunday morning, we got up late and had our Café National in our room. Also read the Paris Herald and got a bit of news.

Then went to Notre Dame. It was so moving. It was a low Mass and no sermon, but a fine organist was at the old organ. He gave us a wonderful treat at the end. When the priest turned to say "Dominus vobiscum" then to give his blessing and we all genuflected, and he went on to the gospel side for the last gospel. Everyone took his thumb and made the sign of the cross on the forehead – bless the mind – on the lips – bless the speech – and the breast – bless the heart. The regular thing, but to see everyone doing it – to realize – here is where de Gaulle reclaimed it for God and France and the World. To hear the lovely music – to roll my eyes over the magnificence of the glass and stone.

Well, it made me begin to cry. I felt it too too something. Finally, we got up and went out. We stopped by the English plaque and dropped a little money in the bag which the nun in her huge white coif held out to us. Then we began to hear the taxis hooting, the French people chu-chutting and the pigeons were still fluttering, the sun still shining. There was the Seine – and we strolled over to the flower market. There it all was. The birds – lovelier than of yore and lots of young ones. Dad said, "I cried too, you weren't the only one bawling." I was glad of it as I felt rather silly.

We had lunch and then visited the Louvre – finer than we remembered. Tea here with a French friend of Dad's. Then to the theater to see "La Folle de

Chaillot". It's a play by Jean Giraudoux and it's a marvel. The costumes were all taken from Paris attics and what a play!

It's all symbolic of the Occupation – the idea is that the old fool (the French aristocracy) gets together with the poor, the deaf, the servants and the police etc. to beat out the businessmen and scientists etc. "who adore the black gold" – oil. Well, those men are the villains who try to seize the poor drowned youth – the young men of France – to enslave them in their plans of making money. To drive them away from the youth the old fool rings a bell – that's publicity of course.

The end is in the bedroom of the old Countess, "La Folle" – she says no man has been in the room in 10 years – well the scene is a wonder. In come other fools, the chic French class, with "Dicky", an imaginary dog – in comes the other fool, a religious type hung with scapulars, etc., then the intellectual type, they all join up. So, then they figure out how to beat the devils who are out to enslave the young and seize everything. They get the sewer man, and he makes a passage into the sewers. They get a bottle of oil and scent up everything. Then all the evil ones come, smell the oil and go jumping down into the sewers. The girls who represent the cocos come and follow the men. Then the publicity men come and race after the others. Then the old lady lies down and has a dream. Up from the floor come wraiths – first the Friends of Animals, all in gray gowns and hats, wigs collars of some ancient time. They name themselves and bow. Next come the Friends of Vegetation, next group is the good Friends of Men – the frightened ones who follow the way of least resistance. The ghosts disappear and the crowd – the beggar, the fools etc all come back in and congratulate the Countess (The Madwoman) who has saved them from slavery. The actress is an old woman of about 70, she is a marvel with an excellent voice. In her last speech she announces that now all the French must work hard, be good, marry and have children – and then there will be nothing that a good woman can not fix.

Well, that was a great finish to a great day.

Then today, we had lunch with Mr & Mrs. Bereau at the George V. It was surely a grand affair! So, all in all, here we are!

Love, Mother"

May 7, 1946

The Paris shops are still weak on things to sell. I went to one grand magasin and the shelves were still bare, but I was able to buy some wooden coat hangers for 134 francs apiece.

When we departed from the hotel, I said to the chambermaid here are two dozen coat hangers. You may have them. "But Madam," said she, "don't you want me to keep them for you? I will keep them until you come back again." I said, "Oh that may be for years, or it may be forever." "Never mind, I will keep them for you."

In the same big store, I passed along the household linens.

There I saw some piles of sheets. Last year there were none, so I asked to see them. All they had were heavy handwoven linen of immense length and hand embroidered heavily. Some poor lady had sold her trousseau to the store. I regretted of course that such things were not for me at any price even though $125 was quoted. I just didn't need sheets that much.

All over Paris the windows of the shops have been made a specialty. They no longer depend upon their merchandise for beautiful windows. Hermes for example, has the most fascinating displays. During the war he began to exhibit his beautiful antiques with here and there a pair of gloves, or a bit of leather goods since his shop is supposed to be primarily a leather goods establishment. Nowadays his windows are a topic of conversation. "Have you seen Hermes' windows?"

He puts the most amazing things on show. One window had a piece of yellow satin tacked all over the floor and sides of the show space and over it was spread a lovely black lace shawl. On that a set of antique library steps. On each of the lovely brown, polished wood steps a pair of yellow gloves were standing up with fingers spread out. Another window had sand for a base and a large vase of flowers set to one side, and the scene of the sky and the sea painted by someone with talent. The window served as an immense bird cage, so sparrows flew around or pecked at the sand, and we all stood six deep to admire.

One other shop had big windows painted with a sort of whitewash in a pale blue and white to look like interior walls. Two immense antique gold picture frames were hung outside on the street side. Inside the frame, lighted up from within, were exhibits of the shop looking for all the world like painted still-lifes. Every evening the frames were removed and put inside, and the iron grill let down.

One perfume shop showed an exhibition of antique fans. So, it seems the war brought to an end a display of opulent merchandise and brought about an era of good taste, imagination and pride and tradition.

I am sure there is no other city today where the richness of their past and the greatness of their present are so visible. The French have guarded their traditions. In France you will find people who seem to be quite certain that they are a privileged race. They are glad to be alive first, and second to be French, and third they have no expectations of coming back as ghosts so they try to do what they would like to see done before they die. They are at work like beavers night and day on some pursuit. One woman I know is raising bantam chickens on her time off.

We went to see the woman recommended to us by Madame Elaine Saliou of the Cenocle. Her name is Allard. She waxed eloquent about the whole war experience. Barbed wire in all the subways, and so forth, and Germans everywhere. She was questioned by the Gestapo three times because she was suspected of aiding the Jews. She said she was not afraid.

Just everyone says that they thank us. The man in the paint shop says Roosevelt saved him and his wife. They were slated for extermination and when Roosevelt said he would exterminate an equal number of Germans; they waited and then the war was over, and so he and his wife escaped.

May 8, 1946

Up in time to go over to St, Pierre de Chaillot, for the 7:30 Mass. As we came home a truck of German prisoners passed us going to begin their forced labor. All smiling big smiles. Husky looking men. Such a contrast to the little thin French men streaming along on foot. To see the creatures big and stout and well-fed and riding to work made me feel a little bit funny.

I felt funnier later to read on the front page of the Figaro a bit of news under the title, A Luncheon Missed: "The City of Paris waited, Tuesday, at a luncheon in the Hotel de Lauzun, the Big Four. The Guard of Honor for the affair had dressed themselves in their best with newly made trimmings. The rooms were ornamented with the most beautiful flowers from our Parisian hothouses. The menu was simple, but perfect: Lobster a l'Americain; Roast Chicken; Asparagus; Sauce Florentin; and Strawberries Melba. But the sun, at first full on the Isle of St. Louis, began to slip to the West. Worn out with standing on guard, the soldiers put themselves at "repos." At the Luxembourg, the other side of the Seine, they discussed Trieste, Transylvania. The meeting lasted up until 1:56 exactly the at the Quai d'Anjou. Mr. Felix Gouin invited the personalities present to come to the table. Only one of the Big Four came, Mr. Bidault, but it was after two o'clock." I go now to get my hair washed and Will goes to see Ambassador Caffery. We are to go to a reception this evening for the Big Four and we will be there.

Hotel Claridge, Paris
Dear Bob and Libby,

We will be here until Monday, so please write to us in care of the Hotel de France in Pau from now on. We hope to hear from you soon. We had a letter from Bob on the first day.

You may get this by May 17. If so, do not forget Elise has that appointment at the Boston Guild for the Hard of Hearing, 273 Commonwealth Ave. I hope she gets that aid. She will be much better off with it, I am sure.

We are having such a fine time. All I can complain about is the lack of time. Today we got in about 30 minutes at an art exhibit at the Salon. We both just felt sick – nothing at home begins to touch this lovely stuff. So many beautiful things, it eases aches and all. All is perfectly beautiful. The sculpture is grand, bookcases, just everything. Dad says he can never paint again, it all beats us so.

We went to Molyneux's show. Lovely clothes being shown. Not many, but simple and lovely.

Everywhere things are beautiful. People really are nearly all very hungry. It hurts to see how they limit themselves. They really are all very thin. However, they have never been so charming and so beautifully dressed – it is a marvel.

Our waiter is a boy who used to be on the Normandie. He was made prisoner in the first days of the war and thrown into a slave camp in Stuttgart. They were kept in a corral and marched out each day to work different places. He said he certainly would have died but for packages sent to him from Boston. Some from the Boston Red Cross and others from a bunch of ladies there. He is going to give me the names. I think I will write these good ladies. They would be glad to hear what he says about their boxes.

We are now on our way to a reception the rector is giving for the Big Four. We may see some interesting people and I always love to go to these things. It will keep me up late, but I hope to be able to stand it! We go and come entirely by Metro. I am beginning to learn where I am a bit. No one is allowed to take a taxi with out first asking a Sargent de Ville for permission.

So far so good. I haven't gotten to the nursing subject yet!

Well, love to all of you – give our darlings kisses for BahPa, Granfadder, etc. CDR"

May 9, 1946

Today, up early and to St. Pierre de Chaillot. Afterwards, breakfast. Then to Frances Fox to get the shampoo. Went to Molyneux and got a card. We duly presented ourselves. Everything is grey this year. Smart grey dresses with long full sleeves and pleats in the skirt. Everything practical. The bride's dress very full, all chiffon with the long sleeves, high Basque neck, and short veil. The skirt was just floor length. The veil was of chiffon like the dress, cap shaped top, and in front and up and back with a spray of white lilacs and a rose. The bouquet, two or three white roses and a huge spray of white lilacs. It was all very nice.

Some outfits were attractive. Shoes made of fabric to match the high clogs and this was wound around the ankle.

I ordered a black suit, all plain black with a pleated skirt and a belted effect in the jacket. Saw some friends and took lunch with them at the Ritz on Friday. Dinner late, and then by Metro to the Sorbonne.

All bright with lights and flags — a brilliant affair. The Bevens were there, and we met Molotov. He looked like a secretive little boy. I asked, "Parlez-vous Anglais?" He shook his head. Then I asked, "Parlez-vous Francais?" He shook his head. Then I said to the wife of the ambassador, "How do you say, "How do you do?" in Russian?" She said something like, "Kakoo stilich." I tried it and added, "Americanski." Molotov smiled and we shook hands.

I think the Russians are just farm boys trying not to get gypped. As if it were that simple. It seems clear to me that they are a bunch of boys off the farm and stalling for time. When the League of Nations forms, the good old U.S.S.R. will act just like the U.S.A. did in the previous League. I've a feeling it is a green country. Not used to being part of a leading group, not having any intention of being out-smarted; therefore, just sitting tight.

The rooms were beautiful and in perfect taste. The walls of a pale beige satin brocade. The furniture in the same. The drawing room was in pale blue brocade; on the walls, curtains, sofas, and all of the same, all done in pale blue satin with large bowls of flowers and tapestries hung on the walls.

Champagne was served and other things. We talked French to some and English to others. Later on, we were in the rush hour getting home by Metro.

No taxi can be picked up anywhere In Paris. It is a really good idea. It would do more to putting an end to the "cocos" than anything else.

May 10, 1946

Up early to St. Pierre de Chaillot. They were erecting a catafalque for a big Mass in memory of someone. I think it was for a young girl, 23 years old, who died a year ago in Ravensbrueck concentration camp. She had received the Legion d'Honneur, Croix de Guerre, and so forth. She must have been a real heroine. Her name was Hélène Roederer.

To lunch at the Ritz with the Whitecottons. To the credit of the

Ritz, let it be said the meal was not black-market. There was black bread, hors d'oeuvres of tomatoes and such, a casserole of bea

ns, et cetera, and a bit of meat and bones. The dessert was one of those powdered custards that we are so responsible for, and Café Nationale.

Later on, we came home and rested and then went to the Red Cross headquarters and made plans to do some service with the Red Cross dispensary when I returned. The rooms are very attractive with a huge table of plywood and curtains of white rayon painted with red crosses, and little bouquets of red poppies and blue forget-me-nots. I came home in the rain, and we had tea and dinner with Dr de Breuil.

Saturday May 11, 1946

Up early and took the Metro to go to the Franciscan Convent. We were late and after walking a long distance, Will stayed to see the little First Communicants. I kept on and arrived just after all was over. I missed the Mass and so forth.

The Chapel is beautiful, and all the nuns were there in their white habits. They filled the front part. The Cardinal was there in his red taffeta. The boys in white. The windows were open, and canaries were warbling in the trees in the garden. Peace on earth, good will galore.

After the Recessional I spoke to a nun and was told to go to the loge. There I was shown into a tiny drawing room and there appeared to be many along the corridor. In each one was a table with café au lait set up. I wanted some, it looked so deliciously arranged with old fashioned china pots and pretty cups.

I went back and found Will having coffee at a street cafe near a market where the French were as busy as bees. Home to our own cafe with currant preserves and brioches, very much appreciated, with some butter. I leave the butter. I hope the servants get it. We go to lunch with the Aime Lerois, then dinner with Brillouin.

Now for our trip to the salon. I feel as if I'd been up all day long. The trip in the metro was so long. Coming up to the Etoile we walked down here. The workers were busy putting up stands all around the

Etoile and fencing down the avenues. The children were out in long processions, boys here and girls there, it seems France is to see so they will realize all the work that goes into a grand effect. This is the behind-the-scenes work.

We went to lunch with Aime Leroi. He gave us a tour of Notre Dame. We saw bullet holes all over. The Germans were apparently pretty poor shots. In one place the spots were gouged out all around a small pair of windows. The Gothic twin arches above the two windows were joined by one small sort of column. The column was broken, and even then, they had missed the windows.

We went to the salon and came home by the Etoile where a wreath-laying ceremony was en marche.

We enjoyed seeing it all very much.

The Paris crowd was orderly except for ignoring their national anthem. Home to dinner with Brillouin. We waited about twenty minutes in front of the hotel. The poor chasseur chased taxis until he was in a sweat, but there were none to be had. One man had big bags and was on his way to the train.

We gave up and went to the Metro "n'importe" my tired feet. A lovely dinner with canned turkey from the U.S.A. Charming people and a beautiful apartment on the top floor of a building just behind the Louvre. The Gestapo came two or three times, but the maid just said the master was in the country and would be back in a day or so and nothing was ever disturbed except for one thing — a bomb fell through the ceiling and broke up everything in that room. The one thing that was untouched was a lovely chandelier hanging in the ceiling, all made of clear, light blue Venetian glass and blown to look like a bowl of large, clear-colored tulips, very beautiful and miraculously untouched by the bomb.

May 12, 1946

Home late in the Metro and slept from ten to seven. Up and out to Mass. The Champs Elysees have been swept and set out with wooden fencing and everything ready for the big VE Day parade. Companies of children have already occupied choice benches. One poor little boy, about ten, had a prize seat. He looked thin and eager. I decided to bring him out some hot coffee. When I came back, the bench was taken by about ten teen-aged youths and the poor little early bird had flown.

> ### Big Four's Foreign Ministers See Paris V-E Anniversary Parade
>
> By KENNETH CAMPBELL
> By Wireless to THE NEW YORK TIMES.
>
> PARIS, May 12—Men marching in cold precision, bugles and a lavish display of flags and gold braid marked the celebration of the first anniversary of the end of the Second World War in Europe today. The young King of Cambodia, wearing sky-blue silk knickers, stood with President Félix Gouin and the Big Four's Foreign Ministers to take the salute in the shadow of the Arc de Triomphe.
>
> Intermittent rain took some gleam out of the colorful proceedings but did not dampen the ardor of Parisians, who watched their armed forces carry the Tricolor past the saluting point. M. Gouin, the only speaker, confined himself to ringing generalities about the greatness of the Allies who won the victory. There were cheers for each country and their volume was probably about equally divided. A great burst of applause followed M. Gouin's praise of former President de Gaulle, who was in the Vendée Department honoring the late Georges Clemenceau, the architect of French victory in the First World War.
>
> The Government had declared two days of general festivities, which began last night when the King of Cambodia and the Foreign Ministers appeared to milling thousands as they left the Opéra, which was brilliantly illuminated. Paris danced in the streets last night, but showers dampened the outdoor festivities tonight.
>
> The Arc de Triomphe parade was the most colorful event. The Republican Guards and municipal guards, uniformed, bemedaled and gold-braided, were on hand early with massed music. Bugles and muted drums sent crashing echoes under the arch as M. Gouin laid a wreath on the tomb of the Unknown Soldier and relit the flame.
>
> Before the parade began Secretary of State James F. Byrnes talked lengthily with Foreign Secretary Ernest Bevin, while Foreign Minister Vyacheslav M. Molotov, probably a victim of linguistic difficulties, stood apart, his hands locked behind him. After a considerable number of tanks and other armored vehicles had passed, the real parade began with mounted Republican Guards. A tiny United States Army band then swung down toward the saluting point amid the respectful silence of the huge French field music groups. The American 787th Military Police Battalion went by in creditable order and the valiant sixteen-piece band drew applause.
>
> Other units included a detachment from the Royal Welsh Fusiliers a crack British regiment. The detachment was headed by men wearing traditional white tabards and leading the regimental goat. A detachment of polytechnical cadets marched in their solemn garb, which gives the effect of the dress of the French Academy.
>
> A battalion of French foot chasseurs drew prolonged applause as it went by at its arm-pumping quickstep. Its mellow bugles played hunting calls. Naval and air cadets' detachments from France's battleships, with army units largely formed of rugged young men of the wartime French Forces of the Interior, set the crowd cheering. Moroccan, Algerian and other overseas troops marched with semi-Oriental military music.

NY Times article describing the VE Day Parade
NY Times Archive, May 13, 1946

Troops were taking up their places along the route and we were most interested to watch. Now at 10:00 a.m. the street is filled with two rows of Sergeants de Ville, each in a dignified stance with his red cordon on his shoulder, his rain cape hanging behind, and the white line around the top of his smart cap – very proper.

The street has been swept and sanded. The crowds are talking in an orderly but gay and good way. Low clouds are the signs of rain. The airplanes are flying over.

The band is coming now; drums, blue uniforms, people chatting, the sanders are sanding, St, Cyr flourish of trumpets, flags of the field, some of them just rags, and the men in khaki. Afterwards, men in blue with red plumes in their hats. The street is quiet again and the children of the "Patrie" are going on well up the line. The line of buttons on the fronts of the jackets of the Sergents-de-Ville shine in tiny high spots under the trees. The people in motion on the sidewalks. A Red Cross ambulance is drawn up at the next corner. The American G. I.'s are here and there. Will is sketching the scene.

The parade began about 11:30. Aime Leroi and some other friends have been with us at the window. I invited the femme de chambre and the valet de chambre and the manageress. They all seemed to talk to me at once. I invited them all, with one reservation, "no one can climb over the parapet." Of course, the valet, with a charming smile, immediately climbed up on it. So, I said, "No, not at all, only behind it.

[1] "Big Four Conference" Wikipedia, The Free Encyclopedia, Wikimedia Foundation,16September,2016 https://en.wikipedia.org/wiki/Big_Four_Conference

12

May/June 1946 - South of France

Editor's Introduction: Here, as in some of her earlier writings, Chloe lapses increasingly into French, which is generally understandable from context.

En route to Pau May 13, 1946

We went down to visit a battlefield past the old chateaux dreaming in the midst of fields of golden grain.

We were completely lost and at last we came to a crossroads. Just as we arrived a vision popped out of a hedge before us. A beautiful little lady; she wore high heeled red slippers, a fabulous full skirt of red printed silk and a white blouse and perched on her head was a modish Paris hat. From her shoulder hung a smart, red bag. We stopped her and asked where we could find the battlefield. She told us in detail, and then I said, "Could we take you some of the distance on your route?" "Ah, that would be very nice."

She was on her way to meet a train of troops, men going from one hospital to another. She talked about the hospitalized men. She told about their sufferings that were brought on after long terms in concentration camps and in prison as well as in the underground, and in the battles. She praised the Americans. "I love America," she said. "We were lost without you. We fought for each other, We suffered for you, and you suffered for us. If I had only known you were coming up, I would have received you in my chateau and given you a proper reception. I wish we could lift a glass of Champagne to each other." On and on. We let her out at the station, and she waved us on to the battlefield.

Some hours later on Will said wistfully, "I can still see that beautiful little woman. Who do you think she was? I do wish so much that we could have lifted that glass of Champagne to her." All she left behind were kind thoughts. A very popular guest.

Another hot day. We had just left the home of Jeanne d'Arc. You may have heard of the poor shepherdess. Well, she may have been a shepherdess, but she could hardly have been very poor. The house in which she was born is a large, two story, substantial stone house. In this country we would call her a rich farmer's daughter, well endowed.

As we drove along the sunbaked road, I saw a very old woman and a little girl. The old woman's gray locks shone in the sun, and the child's face could not be seen for a woman's high, black hat. It appeared that the mother was ill, and a great-aunt was taking the child to her home many miles away up and down tremendous hills. The child became overcome with the heat, so the old woman put her hat on the youngster's head. We offered to take them with us. The messenger who had brought the news of the illness had been another niece. We saw her shortly laboring up the hill on her bicycle, and the old woman waved and shouted as we went by. How surprised the poor girl on the bicycle looked to see those she left walking so slowly pass her by in a big machine.

Further on we passed a big field. Two women were at work and looked up as we drove by. Our old woman lifted up her voice shouting "Voyez!" For our benefit she announced "Elle est ma niece."

The poor niece was openmouthed to see the pair she had expected for dinner late in the evening arriving after breakfast. The old woman was also enthusiastic about Americans. Full of sympathy for us because not long before one of our big planes had crashed in a cornfield and no one was saved.

We have just passed through Amboise. Will said the whole country is saying, "Paint me. Paint me." We see fields of red clover in bloom; lovely green fields all like a lovely dream. We can now see the home of the cliff-dwellers. We can see lovely chateaux. Everything is in place and everything in peace.

This is Vouvray. Rusty bolts in piles, Rails. Temporary work. Temporary bridges. Huge rocks. All French workmen. Concrete mixers going slow. The bridge under construction. The river deep and wide, and pieces of Bailey bridge here and there.

In Tours we saw a part of a stone bridge mended with a Bailey bridge and in use.

We have passed Poitiers now. The yellow broom is in bloom along the tracks, and we see the gorse back on the hills. The country has become less lush and beautiful and there has been more bombing, especially around Poitiers.

Pau, May 15, 1946

Up early and walked to St. Josephs. We arrived and the Institutrice arrived and herded the children inside. The bell began to ring and we were... (pages missing)

...so clean and pretty, with a violet scarf tied around her neck. Her home is as clean as could be. Big, black walnut wardrobes, one on each side of the door, shelves inside; two tables, one along the wall for dining, one in the middle of the room for cooking. A small stove against the wall. A large highboy in front of the windows. The whole place neat and clean and polished. Everything painted. Lattices on a green pole. The walls are pink outside.

Our taxi ran on charcoal — gasogene, they call it. It went excellently well. We went to see Mme. Jourly. She is much thinner and much healthier looking, but very badly dressed. She still is rolled up in shawls. We went on again to Lourdes. We felt like homing pigeons. We looked up Mrs. O 'Toole and Mrs. Douly and we found nothing at all changed. Then on to Tarbes. The Peyres were still flourishing and now we go there tomorrow to attend their first fete since the war. It is the first

Communion of the little daughter. Will is already armed with little bracelets and I have a box of candy.

May 16, 1946

We left Pau, loaded into a car and arrived in Tarbes and went into the restaurant by the side door. The main entrance was closed, and the windows were covered with big iron shutters, but inside all was gay. A U-shaped table took up the center of the room. There were baskets of flowers tied with white bows of figured gauze. The flowers were roses and other kinds of white flowers, like the tiny little white garden carnations. The table was set with white linen and dishes and at each place a huge linen napkin, beautifully folded to stand up. We admired everything. We were kissed on both cheeks by everyone.

Then we went to the Jardin Massey and we saw the peacocks strutting about. We saw the magnificent trees – one a cedar of Lebanon brought back by the Crusaders - and met more of the family. We had photos taken. We met little Bernadette and Christiane, both very cute. Bernadette, or Nadette, as she is called is a big, rosy-cheeked child exactly like Papa, all in a long white dress and done up beautifully. Christiane was only a First Communicant, (not fully instructed) she was in a short dress and a short veil. We all returned to the house and began on the aperitifs.

I met the great grand-mere Peyre, a fine, big-boned Frenchwoman of ninety-eight years, bright and well-spoken, her mind is keen. She still runs the "Caisse" at her hotel. She told about knowing Bernadette — St. Bernadette. She said, of course she had no idea that St. Bernadette would do what she did, but all the same she felt everyone knew she was not an ordinary girl. Very quiet, thoughtful, and not fresh at all, but just perfectly normal. She was at the Grotto with her mother the day of the Miracle, and she saw Bernadette talking. She saw but she could not hear what was said. When Bernadette pulled up the herbs and began to eat, her mother saw her, and she said water rose where she pulled up the weeds. Bernadette leaned over and took her hands and caught a few drops and sucked them out of her hands and then leaned down and scooped up the mud and all and smeared it over her face.

The crowd cried out against her then and the great-grand mother Peyre's father gathered Bernadette up in his arms and ran with her to his house to save her, because the crowd would have killed her. Her parents had been beating her nearly senseless to get her to drop the whole thing, so he picked her up and ran across the little bridge to his house. The bridge could be closed, so he closed it and they had to bring Bernadette to because she had fainted. When she came to, she fell on her knees and cried out that she saw the Virgin in the window. It was the last time she ever saw her. She was promised pain and misery all her life, and that she was granted. However, the Apparition promised her relatives happiness and prosperity forever. The grand-mere said, "She has saved us all. She made the fortune of our country. No one is ever poor anymore." The great-grand mere was invited to Rome for the Sanctification and talked with the Pope three or four times. I hope to see her again. She is really a fine old woman. I am so glad she is so bright and clear in her mind.

Lourdes, May 17, 1946
We have now arrived at Lourdes. I would like to remain indefinitely, but we are due in Cauterets on Monday.

Cold and rainy. I was completely under the weather. Later, I got up and went out to paint with Will and followed the Stations of the Cross. People near me all looked very poor. Their stockings darned at the heels and the men in such thin, threadbare clothes, usually much too small for them. Most of the men's shoes, as well as the women's have wooden soles. The leather ones never look solid or good.

A group of pilgrims came from Nantes. It is something to think about. The tears in many eyes, and the sad faces. One young girl went the whole way barefoot, her shoes in her hand.

Another carried her arms out cross-fashion. I noticed the priest who led them. He was a brilliant speaker and gave fine talks. He stressed three of the Stations. He said he had often thought he would liked to have lived at the time of Jesus. He would love to have visited in His home for a meal, and so forth, or to be there when He was an infant in the manger, but now, he said, after all he had seen of life, and the German Occupation, he would rather be with Christ on the Chemin de Croix and to have helped Simon the Cyrenean when he attempted to help Jesus Christ carry his Cross.

I felt that he no doubt had helped these people to carry their crosses during the war. He said, "Nous Francais, nous sommes un people discipliné...I want you to divide into two files and separate as you come out of the gate, then we will go down to the statue of the Virgin for our last prayers." There, he called upon us all to pray that we all may be uplifted. I prayed hard myself, and as it was finished, and we turned away I saw most everyone weeping. What dreadful times they have had. Mme Peyre's tales about the Gestapo no doubt would be pale alongside the poor people of Nantes.

It was there that the poor French tried to aid the commandos and were killed by the hundreds, there that the Germans were really entrenched and held out to the very last moment. I feel the people show it; they look so poor and so beaten. I pray they may receive blessings of kindness and love and true signs that God, indeed, loves them.

We met an old Irish priest, and an American girl from South Dakota. She wants me to look her up in Paris. The old priest was very funny. He told about the Yankees who took stickers off the luggage to sell to others.

He also told about being out in Australia when someone told him to keep his hands in his pockets. He asked why, and they said, "These fellows are larrickin' 'round." What does "larricking" mean? Evidently it is having fun with the girls, so it all boils down to nothing.

Dr. Nicholau brought a young man named Cazenave, head of the Resistance here. He said this hotel was their center. A young American man lived here and helped all the time. The boys left by the Pass of Estom. All other ways could be too well watched, but Estom was too big to cover fully.

Friday, May 18, 1946

We are up and about and it is a beautiful morning. Will's birthday. We plan to paint. This house was owned by a man who did big things in the last war. The Germans came and took him away at the very beginning of the war and he died in prison in Germany. His children run the house with an excellent staff, two very young girls about seventeen and nineteen. The son is about twenty-one. His face is so sad and tragic that he is hardly the one to greet people at the door. Everyone is so kind. They want us to be pleased so much it makes us feel as if we were more blessed in all ways more than we could ever deserve.

Kneeling in the Crypt I looked around at all the beautiful work in the walls; whether the tiles or marble or the carving, it is all a revelation. No one except a savage could fail to feel that everyone strained his very nerves to build it and maintain it.

For five long years they have lived on hope alone here. Now they seem like a people who are strong. No one seems weak or silly. But this is a place where people come for a purpose and not to relax.

Bob with his children Bobbie & Torrie, Christmas 1945
Russell Family Archives

"Hotel Gallia et Londres, Lourdes, May 18, 1946
Dear Bob,

Dad and I keep thinking of you here – everything is something "le grand petit Robert" did or said.

We attended the first communion celebration of the daughter of Bernadette, they call her Nadette. It was with the Peyres. It was such a swell occasion; I wish you had been there. It was your picture with Torrie and Bobby that stole the show.

Of course, the younger men had all been in prison or slave camps in Germany. The older ones had been taken up before the Gestapo, etc. Mme Peyre had just stayed in her room with her two little girls. The father-in-law ran the restaurant, and one half was taken over for the German officers, so they had the fat of the land to eat, but upstairs was the Gestapo. Madame said she could take everything but that – she said she nearly lost her mind when she saw boys she knew dragged up the stairs and heard the cries and the thumping of blows. She said, "Mercifully, they usually died!" Isn't it awful?

The family of the Peyre's is the family that rescued St. Bernadette from the crowd and from her parents when everyone wanted to lynch her. Their family name is Nicolau and they were promised every blessing. They have everything as far as comfort there is in the world. They are fantastically religious and good – so no wonder they were so kind to us when we arrived with Bill in that awful crisis with his asthma.

I went the way of the cross with a huge pilgrimage from Nantes. There was a fine man leading them. He gave a little talk at each station. When he came to the one where Simon the Cyrenean helped Christ to carry his cross, he said he had often wished to live during the time of Christ – like any other boy in his home etc. However, he said "how after all that has happened, I feel I would rather be with Simon – when he helped Christ to bear the cross"

It is still the same old place. Shoes all have wooden soles and begin to claque about 5 am. There are still swarms of pilgrims sick and well. Also, it is awful to recall that the Patron of this hotel was taken by the Gestapo in the first days. He died at Ravensbrook. His three children all own the house, and all are under 21.

How is darling Torrie and how is little Erland – and my dearest friend

Bobby – tell him I have bought him a nice pair of Lourdes socks all made by hand and bright red!

Well, do write us at the Hotel Chalet up in Cauterets. We will be there for three weeks.

Love, Mother"

Sunday, May 19, 1946

We took the trip to Gavarnie, today. Last night I made my trip in the procession and drank the water of the Grotto. Also, about six o'clock Will and I wandered up to the top of the hill and took the beautiful path through the woods and down to the Grotto along the river. There were two men fishing, standing in the stream, casting. Velvety green hills rolled up and away and the white cows grazed on the hillsides.

Beautiful farmhouses were shuttered, pink and cream in the sunshine. We could see a man coasting in on a bicycle, so we knew people were at home. The river, the Gave roared, and the rushing of the waves made us dizzy, so we set out for home and dinner.

Going on the trip to Gavarnie we had a rickety old bus, but it ran well. The driver looked like Jay. He, too, wore a coat of a little boy. The thing I noticed most about the men is that they all wear clothes much too small for them. Thin little coats well above their fat bottoms. I suppose they could only buy 14-year-old size or some such thing. Today, in church, a girl came in wearing a pair of pale-yellow slippers with pointed toes and French heels. They looked like some that belonged to my aunt, worn fifty years ago. I think she had undoubtedly found them in the attic.

Gavarnie was more beautiful than I remembered it. The lovely hills, so green, crowned by the distant frosty beauty of miles and miles of snow and deep shadows and gorges and glaciers stretch up like a huge backdrop to a theater. The air was bracing, invigorating, and cold. Two young men in the bus with us dressed neatly, and they set out to walk that path to the Refuge. The mud was just like it used to be, but the price a mule ride of 200 francs was too steep. The pilgrims are usually poor people. I wish Gavarnie would clean up that mudhole so the poor people can walk clean and well shod and not be obliged to climb or get filthy, or else ride a horse or a mule and pay 200 francs.

We had tea at the little tea shop we used to patronize. The woman in charge talked about the Allemands. She told about the digging out of "Notre Henri". His handsome, big, bronze bust was cast into the cannon molds and it seems a shame that this tiny hamlet should have been deprived of its one monument, and for such a small amount of bronze, such a lot of trouble. It seemed like a personal affair to Will and me.

Monday, May 20, 1946

Today, up and out to the Grotto. Not quite so cold. My pink sweater and two Canadian sweaters and heavy Navy winter suit and heavy Navy overcoat were enough to keep me warm today. I slept all night without my heavy quilt. Up until now I have been nearly asleep with the cold all day long, and no coffee or tea to buy. Each morning I ask for boiling water and use some of my teabags. I asked the neat, little waitress if she wanted one, and she said, "Oui-i. Les Espagnoles aiment le thé." So, I discovered she is Spanish. She has lovely blue eyes and black hair and makes me think of the beautiful wife of the man in New York, Theodata O'Reilly, an Italian girl married to an Irishman, representative in New York of the Duveen house. I met her years ago with Professor Hendricks.

Chloe in her hiking clothes in the Pyrenees
Russell Family Archives

May 21, 1946

We arrived in Cauterets by car. At Lourdes we went out to buy a pot to boil our water, and two cups, and a few cherries and lemons to take with us. Will got me some candy, the famous Berlingots at the same old place, where the proprietress said, "Les bon bons sont bons. Noblesse oblige." when she did them up so exquisitely, just as so long ago, in 1937. Today we got very few, and they were very dear. She said she had been taken up by the Germans. She was "denoncé par un anonyme" - who, she never knew. They gave her a going-over but did not imprison her. Her eyes had such a strange light, it seemed to me as if she were saying, "But I did help the boys all the same."

Everywhere people say the same thing, "Les Boches. Ils sont les diables." Everyone seems to have been revolted by them.

We took hot baths at the Bains de Cesar. The same old woman was there. She, too, spoke about the old times and the Germans. She said she had "un tres mauvais experience." The hotel was occupied. Also, the Hotel Pont d'Espagne. So very few men escaped through here. The Hotel Angleterre was used as a place for convalescents, particularly German children.

Tuesday May 21, 1946

We walked up to the Hotelerie de la Reine Hortense. It was higher than I remembered, but I made it easily. We sat and sketched in the rain, and then came home. Went up to the Pont d'Espagne, via autobus after lunch. The woods were being cut out. All of the beautiful big trees and piles and piles of firewood. It used to be that they had coal brought up from elsewhere, but now they are just doing work in the woods.

When we arrived at the Pont d'Espagne we were surprised to see a sentry box and a big barbed-wire entanglement that had served the Germans. They had used swirls of wire simply everywhere, up and down the gorge, and up all along the route to Vallon, it was stretched everywhere.

Mr. Jorly was taken prisoner and sent to Germany. He got ill and was sent home and when he got here they told him he was to keep the hotel open winter and summer. They put him in charge. He had to do as they said, but all he did was run the hotel part. They had their own cook and took care of themselves. He is doing very well now, and it looks as if he is to have a good year.

They also told how they were terribly excited by D-day and said, "Now you will see. The U.S.A. is rich. When she is in, you will be beaten. She said they were furious but did nothing except yell and try to argue. Then, in October, they were told to leave, by the Maquis, from Lourdes, and they all left, just like frightened sheep. She said, "Ils sont des moutons"

There was a fire across the road and a 12-year old child waved them to a stop. They stopped. The child told them to descend and go into the building and they did. He had a note to read to them that they must surrender in 10 minutes. The 10 minutes passed, then an armored tank car with machine guns drove up to the door. The German commander put his hands up over his head and walked out and said he and his men were surrendering. Then they all put their guns and so forth on the table and the 12-year-old child received their surrender.

It was stated by them, however, that the reason they gave up was because Lourdes was a sacred place, and they would not fight there. They had already told everyone up here that there were "60,000 Maquis waiting to kill them."

The Jourly's brought out a glass of wine for Will, and they opened a nice red and white and blue linen cloth on the zinc top of the kitchen table and served us slices of the local ham, and bread.

The handsome, big, chef's stove was going fine, and a maid sat in the other room sorting postal cards, and the herdsmen stood in the door holding little nine-month-old Christian, a darling, bright boy baby. Our friend of years past, Mr. Ziegler, was the main spy hereabouts. He had reported everything, and when Mr. Jorly was called in to be questioned, the German officer had the most exquisitely perfect maps. He had taken the maps of the caves and the refuges. They asked him this and that and then put down their calipers and figured a bit and asked how far it was from here to there, then verified it on the maps that Mr. Ziegler had spent all that time making.

They knew just where to put the barbed wire swirls. They knew everything - the places no one could pass were not guarded. I remembered the fine photographs and photography equipment that Mr.

Ziegler had. Everything was done down to feet and inches. The maps belonging to Meillon could not be bought here in France at all; Zeigler had bought them all.

I gave the little boy my cane and he held onto it and seemed pleased. When his bottle was warmed and given to him, he wouldn't let it go. He wanted to pay attention to us, not his bottle. First, his mother struggled with him, and then she gave him to the herdsman, and he kept plugging until Christian ate most of it. We selected postal cards and soon took the busses back to Cauterets.

May 22, 1946

We went up to the Ferme Basque. The path was very damp, and seven years' growth has had a real effect on the beeches and hemlocks. Huge ferns and light green moss covered the hillside. We followed the path looking up and down through the trees. We came out by the falls, and they were so wild and full of water. We stood on the bridge and watched until we were dizzy, then we went on to the house. It was raining hard. When we knocked, the daughter came out, her poor paralyzed foot in a tan colored espadrille, bare legs, black dress, bobbed hair, sparkling dark eyes, intelligent and sensitive face. She welcomed us warmly. I stood in the hall on the tile floor and stared at the handsome old grandfather's clock on the landing on the stairs. It was banjo-shaped, and the entire thing was one enormous pendulum of bright brass, all repousse figures.

At the bottom, or the largest part, were two figures of a man and a woman. They ride up and down on a seesaw. The face was beautiful, set out with the seasons. The base of fine, Inlaid wood and has a flower design. I asked how long it had been there, and the girl said, always.

We entered the living room; the stone floor, the big fireplace with the small stove inside, the grandmother sat at her knitting inside the fireplace, close to the stove. She looked very old, had few teeth, almost no hair, but was a large woman, and must have been very forceful in her youth. She had bright, black eyes and wanted to talk. They both wanted to talk, so I tried starting them. Before long, both were talking at once and I was agreeing so hard we were all yelling.

They said the Germans were hard workers, they liked to work. They kept very neat and proper. They were very polite and disciplined. They came for tea and sat up straight and proud. Then as they left, they picked up the chair they had used and put it back where it came from. They had to stand guard all winter in big storms, and so when she saw them standing out there in the blizzard, she invited them to come in to warm by the fire. "Comme un bete." Like a beast. They came in and sat down and at once turned on the radio.

They were so wild with joy when the Germans left so swiftly that they both had taken the Pilgrimage to Lourdes. They made the Way of the Cross up over the hill. And they waxed so enthusiastic, and with that poor club foot and the poor grandmother hardly able to move, I couldn't keep from thinking of what Bill said, "The thing Lourdes does for you is show you so many other people so much worse off than yourself that you get better." They had enjoyed their Pilgrimage. The girl said, "Some people say the French peasants are Communists. Not at all. We love our Church. We love to go to Mass. We love to make our Pilgrimage, for then it is just as if it were medieval times. Her eyes shone, and her life was one dazzling excitement to her as she looked forward to Mass on Sunday, a trip to Lourdes once in a while, and so forth.

I told her I was with her.

May 24, 1946

Today we sat and sketched in the Regences until lunchtime. Then we went up to the Ferme Basque. We made sketches of the scene. I am not pleased. Put in too strong a blue. We had tea at the table in the big room. The women were horrified to have us use no tablecloth. They brought out cups and saucers and spoons and clean linen tablecloths. We drank our tea and ate our bread, and we were able to make tea and it was very good, with lemon. We usually take a lemon along and a little box of sandwiches.

There was great talk about the Germans. One was so gentle; he had a chateau and he showed them the picture of it and the picture of his wife and two children. He loved to come up and visit with them. He was a fine painter and painted the portrait of the elderly aunt. Her white hair, her place in the corner by the fire, and so forth. He was a fine man. Of course, he hated war, and Will said, "Je suppose que le diable dirait la meme chose, s'il vous faisait une visite." The women looked worried and then the younger one laughed and said, "Yes, no doubt."

Mathilde had gone to the Fair at Tarbes to buy some new animals. We met her as we went up to sketch in the woods on Saturday. She said she had bought a horse. It came from Canada and is a fine bete. Her little pony is so intelligent. She just sits on its back in a sort of cradle with places on each side for the big milk jugs, or gallon cans, and he goes peacefully at his own will.

She stopped him to chat with us, then said, "Venez, Vilson." Then she explained that he is twenty years old and was named "Vilson - Voodrow Vilson." I said, "Now the new one will be Roosevelt, will he not?" She looked doubtful and said she thought she would call him "Creaky." She stopped to look at our pictures on Monday and said that painting must be a very agreeable pastime. Then, to quote her, "But one must have leisure." I said, "Yes, indeed." The little nun from the school came all the way up to the to thank us for the chocolate. Mrs. Jean-Marie had turned it over to her. She said each child had a morsel. I'm going to take some tea and peanut butter and so forth to her.

Today I saw a little girl, very thin, wearing big mountain boots, very much too big for her. At least she has on shoes, but she needs food and shoes that fit.

Today is Wednesday. We had baths at the Bains de Cesar and now we are sitting, just enjoying this sweet place. We both hate to leave. They gave us our bill the other day, addressed to the Viscount William Russell. Being an American doesn't mean a thing here. We have missed Mass all of the three Rogation Days. I hope not to miss again, I was awake this morning, but felt too lazy to brave the pain of a cold, early morning.

Friday, May 31

Today is St. Petronella's Day. First Communion Day. The church was beautiful with big vases of pale yellow and green leaves, as well as roses here and there in a single vase on the altar. The Bishop's red canopy and kneeling bench were all laid out for his coming for the Confirmation. The children, wearing white wreathes, sat in front. Of course, the boys had no wreathes. The boys with their arms folded and very well behaved. The Sisters of Charity from orphanage were there, their big, white linen coifs as starched and white as if soap were no difficulty here. There were about ten of them and the old church looked so right with them going up the aisle.

We came home and heard that the client next door is very ill. She's the mother of the Mother Superior and she is eighty-some. This is her second stroke. The Cure says, "Of course there is the age." We painted chiefly, today. My arm is much better.

Jean-Marie's sister came down to the place with the baby. She looked perfectly beautiful in a set of pink cushions, sheets, pillow-cases, et cetera, very fine hem-stitching. Her outfit was all pink wool and edged in white angora. She was bawling a mile a minute. Her great-grandmother said she was too hot. She looked very pretty, and I think she was done up to show me how pretty she was, but she was bawling before I could appreciate her.

We got some espadrilles for me. The same shop, all the same except the woman is now a widow and the Cordonnier, who used to work in the window, is gone. She was rather eloquent about the Germans. She said she just looked the other way when they went by. However, morally, she said it was a horrible experience, always to be hating, lying, and so forth, and even to be thinking so as to feel full of hateful ideas.

Sunday, June 21, 1946

We went to the 8:00 o'clock Mass and arrived just as the Cure was coming in, He put on the electric lights on the columns. Tout le monde came. One old man in a lovely, big, black cape. Very handsome. Tall and white haired. Two tiny men took seats beside him, so funny and so small. All white haired.

We drove to Pont d'Espagne and started out for Marque a Dieu. A thick mist and a cold wind was blowing. In spite of that I grew very warm and had to change into my cotton blouse. We passed many fishermen. They didn't all look French. I believe they were German prisoners without their drab suits with the big white PW on the seat of the trousers. The barbed wire installations are all still there. They are whirling, swirling up through the mountains and the small herds of cows look very thin. Little black bulls were brought in to help out with succession, and it is funny to see the number of black sheep as well. The lovely white cows are doomed, I suppose.

We came out of the mist into the bright sunlight, and as we climbed the escalier we recalled a former trip. It seemed to me I could see Jean-Marie and hear his voice; He was telling us how to walk and was smiling. We went on up the final big pull. I leaned against the big rock and admired the handsome pine tree, its roots climbing in and out the rocks all over the road. We arrived in the big park and saw the cows lying on the green grass in the sunshine. We could see the shepherd's house, all newly done up and solid looking. We stopped to look everything over, then when the bridge came into sight we began to climb and the last hard pull up I felt I could see a German soldier come around the rock and he seemed to be saying, "Look and see what we have done." I looked at the big hostel added to the old one. It is big and imposing and has a portico, and then I cast my eyes around and down in the stream is a dam. The German seemed to indicate that that was what he meant. I began to laugh very loud, and he disappeared at once.

So once again we came to the Refuge and we were so thankful to have that supreme delight granted to us once more in this world, to show that the Germans were fleeting things.

June 4, 1946

Yesterday, we went up on the mountain to paint my souvenir. When we came down Mme. La Tapis was just going down to do some errands with the baby, and she began to tell us about Jean-Marie. I told her Bob wanted the whole story, so she told me all she knew. She told about his son coming in anxious at about five o'clock. She had expected Jean-Marie for tea. He always came for tea. He would tease her daughter because she cut the bread so thin. He liked his bread toasted like the English. "Pain grille comme les Anglais." He came every day. That day he did not come. She sent his son to look in the cafes, but he was not there.

At eight o'clock she started out with her son-in-law and several others, and they took the Grande Route. When they neared the Refuge, she saw some firewood on the road. Nearby lay a big rock, and she was sure the wood had been laid out by Jean-Marie; as he always fixed it in a certain way. They would get some small wood and put it on top and drag the whole thing. That was his way of bringing down the wood.

This time he could not be found. His dog had died, so no one knew even where he had gone. She was determined that this was the place. Everyone searched. Men got big, electric torches; others carried lanterns.

Calling Card of Jean-Marie Bordenave, mountain guide of Cauterets
Russell Family Archives

They searched until about nine and she came home and then got a big thermos of coffee and a bottle of rum and went to the doctor and asked him not to go to bed. They got the stretchers and blankets and sheets and so forth and started out once more. They climbed the hillside, but nothing. They were home at 3:00 am and out again at five. Up to the top and down.

At eleven she made some more coffee, and they all began again, six men on one side and six on the other, a systematic search of every inch. Nothing. After lunch, they returned and after 1:30 she said they must go up again, So the exhausted men started. In a few moments, there was a cry. They had found him. He was dead, of course. He had been struck by a big stone. It seemed that he must have heard it, for it hit him in the face, as if he had looked up. Apparently, he had fallen on his head, as the back of his head was crushed. However, he had risen, had composed himself, had the good side of his face cupped in his hand and lay as if in sleep. He had covered himself well with his coat, which was the tan guide's coat, and that is what caused him to fade into the hillside so that he could not be found. He was not far away.

Lourdes, June 8, 1946

We spent the last few days at Cauterets doing the usual agreeable things. At our hotel, three deaths occurred. The grandmother of the Mother Superior, who had her second stroke, but was so strong as to take a week dying. The sudden death of the little Renee, the femme de chambre. Then the death of another relative. The church was all decked out in black velvet with silver galloons and crosses and a big drapery went all around the wall behind the altar, Then the altar rail was hung with it, and the catafalque was draped with it. Everyone was there in deep black, even the big, fine-looking peasant woman who brings the milk into the village each morning. The wheezy, sweet little organ was well-played, and a good choir of the men sang the Mass.

In every way, the whole town was in respectful mourning.

Also, the Hotel de Ville, was very coquette. The awnings were being hung on the Casino and the cafe at the corner, and the dear little tea shop was all set up with its red velvet bancs and the light fixtures were being put in place. The awnings were hung. The girls in the Casino gallery had everything laid out and were ready to serve ices and cakes, and so forth, if any. It all looked delicious, and we hated to leave.

We went for a last day's visit and called on Mme. Vordonov. Her son was there, a smiling handsome lad. He was taken as a slave in Wiesbaden. He said it was a lovely place, but what people! His mother looks ill, but she insisted taking us up to the convent to meet the nuns. The Mother Superior met us. She was just coming out to direct a big truck up the narrow street to deliver something. She had taken off her street habit of enormous black cape and hood and looked exquisite with a white headdress and white apron and sleeves turned back.

She insisted upon showing us into her parlor and wanted to know all about the peanut butter. It was the "vitamins," "Where did we get the cacouettes, etc." Very agreeable. We did not stay long.

So here we are in Lourdes again. We went to the Grotto and sat quietly. It was entrancing. It was a terribly hot day. Today we went to the Mass Communion and then to the Grotto. Mass out of doors and Communion as well. Much the most agreeable place.

June 10, 1946, Tuesday

Yesterday we went to Orleans. It rained hard as we approached the Eglise de Saint Marie. We entered the ancient porch over a big puddle. Many men were there and an elaborate hearse with plumed horses and a driver, the drivers on the box under a big black umbrella. We entered the dim old church and found a crowd assembled and Mass en train. A fine old voice was chanting the old chants. I thought it might be the Monseigneur, but he was nowhere in sight. When we became accustomed to the dimness, we saw him kneeling in the Chancel. After taking off our dripping raincoats and getting a seat in the back, we were much interested to watch. Finally, after many of the men left for a smoke, or a chat, and came back for the touching of the saint's relic, am old woman came close to me and looked at me in a forbidding sort of way. I suddenly realized that a big rope hung beside me. I moved aside and she took the rope, and we soon heard the bell tolling.

The old Monseigneur came up the aisle chanting. Before him, four red-faced porters carrying the plain pine casket with the black velvet cover piled on top. They passed, then the Crucifix, then the Monseigneur, then all the mourners in a long file. I went to pick up my coat to go out into the procession and to leave the church. Suddenly, as we turned, Monseigneur came back into the church and started up the side aisle. We went up to him and addressed him. He was enchanted to meet us, and very much touched to hear why we had come.

He begged us to excuse him as his domestic was ill, but there was a "toute petite coin" in which to eat. Would we give him the honor to dejeuner with him? We would and we did, and what a delicious time. A small Basque restaurant, spotlessly clean. We entered a neat hall with clean red and yellow tiles. Beyond, we could see young boys playing pelota. We were guided into the restaurant. Could Madame provide a dejeuner? Indeed, she could. Soup, hors d'oeuvres, truite, canard de la campagne, fromage de la campagne, bon bons de la campagne, of honey and chopped nuts, and cafe, cognac, and a lovely bottle of wine. This was made at the farm of the proprietors. It was like a dream. We discussed the portico of the church and all sorts of interesting things.

Got at last to the Germans.

They were not mechant at Eau Laurent. When they came, the officer came at once to call on Monseigneur. He wanted to see Sainte Marie as the same architect had built the Augsberg Cathedral where he came from, of course, and he raved about the church and was on good terms with the Monseigneur all during the occupation. When they left they all just disappeared, he said.

He allowed us to sketch in the Eglise and accompanied us to the station dressed in his soutane with the fleece lining and showing as he raised his hand when he drank a toast to us at luncheon. Not only the fleece showed, but a red silk lining as well. His flat black derby hat and his big chin, cool blue eyes and handsome nose and good feet make him seem young, indeed; however, his sunken frame and sunken cheeks and the demeanor of walking gently showed him to be eighty-one, which is what he says he is. What a fine old man and a beautiful church and a joyous luncheon. What a place to come back to.

We boarded the train on time after threading our way through the big Cirque, all set up before the railroad station. Tout Eau Laurent was there, and we were terrified to see some small boys laughing and hanging out of a whirling chair. We all felt sick, and Monseigneur kept saying, "c'est fou!" When he bade us good-bye, he said he must give

Will the accolade and he kissed him on both cheeks, then he said, "Et vous, Madame, il faut dire adieu. I said, "Nay. Je vous dis au revoir." He said, "Eh bien. Je vais dire au revoir. J'espère de vous recontre au delà." Meaning, "Very well, I will say au revoir. I hope to meet you over there." Meaning in heaven.

June 11, 1946, Tuesday at Pau

We took the taxi to Bielle, today, and drove through the old, crooked streets, and past the old church, on up to Bilheres. As we started up the hill the lacets were walled on either side, the gutters made by small, round stones. Then one wall became the retainer to the terracing. There were so many roads criss-crossing from one side to the other that it was a perfect maze. Every road was ancient, covered with lichen and the small round stones carefully laid in rows and patterns. They extended for miles. It must once have been a big city with myriads of streets, for so much work surely means many people.

Now there are very few houses, but roads are used by the sheep and the cows, and here and there the horses with carts. We followed along on and on and up in the green fields, then to a sort of a cross-roads. An old woman in a tiny white cap sat in a window with a distaff. She was spinning a thread from a big hunk of wool. We passed on out on a sort of a plateau and all the time in low gear. We went on, finally arriving at the tiny chapel of Notre Dame de Houndas. There we descended and took our paints and climbed up to the Druid's hill and settled down to sketch.

It grew colder and a mist settled down. A shepherd came over the fields with a number of sheep with the bells. We could see large flocks in two or three neighboring districts. Cows and horses grazed not far away. We felt, at the same time, in the most isolated spot, in full view of thousands, chiefly animals. The big oaks were much the worse for the eleven years since we had seen them. However, we sketched two or three of them. Finally, we decided it was time for lunch and we came down to Bilheres and lunched in the same cafe as years ago.

The wife of the proprietor served us an excellent lunch. Her husband was killed by the Germans for helping parachutists. I said I wanted to send something to her grandchildren. They are very nice children, three of them: Pierre, nine; Annamarie, six; Jean Louis, eighteen months.

We left there and went to Beon to see the old, ruined chateau beside the stream. Still as lovely as ever. We sketched then and started home. We stopped a moment by the stream to see some men fishing. Next, we looked in a little garden and saw some men skinning a dead lamb. We said some "bon soupe!" was coming along there.

We drove on to Pau, our driver talking about his work in the Resistance. He drove an ambulance. Did operations and so forth for the Maquis. He went with a doctor from Pau and worked twenty-three hours daily for a month. Once he was arrested when he had "abuses" under the seat. He was taken in for questioning, and later released. He was arrested by the French and made to stand for 45 minutes with hands in the air. He was let go. He is an excellent man, and it was a pleasure to have such a driver.

Hotel de France, Pau June 12, 1946, Wednesday

Today we walked to the big church through the neat little gardens. The church was dim and beautiful, with just a faithful few, A very bent little old woman crept along the lovely Promenade des Anglais, close to us. I saw her in a corner near the door. She was at the end of the railing for Communion and was still there and creeping back to her seat when we left. The whole place must be such a peaceful, wonderful place to go to Mass, early morning, all winter.

13

July 1946 - Paris

Editor's Note: Much of this chapter consists of chatty references to cultural aspects of the time, and amazingly some things never seem to change – inflation, increasing use of alcohol and rising temperatures.

June 27, 1946, Thursday

Today we went to the Church of the Madeleine, it was Fete de Dieu and there was music; a full High Mass with three priests; music with two organs, all topped off with a procession. We left by a side door and followed more little corridors and winding stairs. What a really great thing a great church is. We came home to have lunch with the R__. Then we set out for the Athenae and we had the great pleasure of seeing La Folle de Chaillot once more.

We woke up late after a late evening and we went to hear C__. It was a fine concert In La Salle Pleyelle. We were happy to hear him at home and he was happy, too. He seemed to give all he had.

We spent the morning at the hospital. Doctor De Breieulle had three cases. One, a young boy of fifteen years with calcification of the heart. I want to send some Christmas presents to the children. I hope to do it for those in the Clinique, and for those in Cauterets. To start out early and see two workmen going to work around the Place de la Concorde, on bicycles, is one of the great pleasures. The silhouette of Paris is now a girl on a bicycle, with a flaring, plaid skirt, tailored jacket, cloth shoes and bag hanging over the shoulder.

The man's silhouette is a man on a bicycle with two big suitcases on the handlebars, and a mountain sack behind. No beret, dressed in tan with pants in tight winds at the ankles.

The big couriers have the baskets with their names on the side and the riders are in uniform with the name in gold on the cap.

Madame __ came to lunch. The poor woman, she has great courage and intends to go on as she is. She has a car and goes and comes all she likes.

Today, I stopped in a little shop, and what a burst about the Germans. The Gestapo had been just across the street. The day of liberation, the Americans came there and took over just in time. In a tiny room, fourteen people with some tiny children, were in a space like a small closet. They had all been locked in and were not able to move. There was a tiny aperture of a few inches, just enough for one to gasp in a few breaths. One at a time, they were helped up by the others, making a little bit of space and giving a few gasps for air, one at a time, hour after hour, they kept at it. When the Americans came, they burst open the door and all the people fell on the floor, but they all lived.

In the baths, it was the same. They put people in tanks of water, and the poor things had no space to swim and nothing to clutch. All they could do was tread water, and they could only keep it up so long. When the Americans came, they saved some in the tanks, also. I bought a washcloth for sixty cents, and I was glad to get it.

June 28, 1946, Friday

The cotton goods do not exist anymore, it seems. Today we had art lessons. Miss ___ started Will by making him mix his paint first and put it on thick, in long, gentle sequences. He is inclined to take it on his brush in a hunk and stab it roughly with no follow-up. The art, of course, lies in the follow-up of the stroke, not in another stab.

We will give a dinner sometime soon.

July 1, 1946, Monday

We went to the ten o'clock Mass at Notre Dame.

The organs, both big and little; the choir boys all in their white linen; the old priests with pale blue stole and silvery hair, sea ted in the old stalls; the light in the rose-windows and just everything so eternal-feeling. We took a taxi and had a drive in the Bois de Boulogne. Saw the Chalet au Lac and the crowds landing on the island, no longer in the old rowboats, but in a big motor launch. Literally millions of people in the Bois.

We sat in one of the beautiful cafes and watched Papa and Maman go by on bicycles, with the young ones in carts tied behind the bicycles, sometimes in tandems with little children on a seat in between.

Home in the Metro to lunch at the hotel, then to the Longchamps with the Whitecottons. They have their car here. I'm so allergic to crowds, it was all I could do to take it, but I managed to keep my temper. Mr. Whitecotton got in a line a mile long, and we stood and stood and stood, and finally a sort of fight commenced. They had to get the Sargeant de Ville to straighten it out. Mr. Whitecotton was knocked out of line three or four times, but he finally came out with some tickets. His face was crimson, and he was in a rage. A French girl who had been in front of him was fainting - what a silly thing. But we finally got places on the top of the stands, and we saw very well, but some other people crowded us out, more and more. A Frenchman in front of us wanted to soothe Mr. Whitecotton. He was so sweet and kind. He wanted to give them his place, but Mr. Whitecotton just stood and was mad. Finally, after the race was run, it turned out that Dad, by accident, had bought the wrong tickets, but the wrong ticket won, so Mr. Whitecotton began to smile and feel good again. What children we all are! And we hate to be pushed around.

Today, I looked around most of the day. Robert Barra came to lunch. He had spent a long time waiting for us in the Cafe Triomphe. It is so important to enunciate clearly such things as they always say "Hotel Crillon" and "Le Triomphe" for the cafe. Will had said "Le Crillon" and it sounded like "Le Triomphe" That was too bad. However, we had a nice visit. He came to take me to Mass at the Benedictines, to hear the Gregorian chant on Friday.

We went to dinner at the Embassy. Dad's suit was perfect, and I wore my black taffeta with the jacket. I pinned a white rose on my chest and wore some of the lovely white sea-shell earrings that I bought, so I looked all right, I've no doubt. The company was large, about fifty of us, I believe. Mostly a group of Southerners. The young woman who was doing the honors was a sturdy, homely little woman with a deep voice.

Much political maneuvering - the type that we think of. She made a fuss, crying out all about "these Russells," because there were others present called Donald Russell and his assistant. She is the daughter of Alben Barkley, the Senator from Kentucky. I liked them all very much. The others were the Hills, the Mexican Ambassador, the Paraguayan Ambassador, and younger embassy people. They all acted as if they thought the French were an inferior race of people and they seemed to wallow in luxury.

I feel so annoyed when they started to tell me who collaborated, and I can't keep from saying, "so did we." Lots of this group seemed to feel very distant from the plain, little Frenchman.

However, it was a good evening, and we had an interesting time.

It is very hot today. We went to L'Eglise Madeleine. Miss ___ came, and we made a real start on Will's rose. I walked out with her and we settled on a little scene for me to do by the river. The heat is making a record. The American paper says 95°. The English 93°. Anyway, both are hot!

The English paper gave me a lot of laughs.

They refer to Hollywood as the Land of Milk and Honey. The American films arrived here today. Mayor LaGuardia says there is a "Purple Market." Much more legal than a Black Market, and the faces of the Congressmen should be red. The inflation grows on in New York, and they say inflation is a fate worse than debt! Everyone is going on vacations to the shore and to take the Baths. The shopgirls' slogan is "Annie get your fun." Drinking is going up, particularly among the women. The men sing, "Come to Me, My Alcoholic Baby." As for the political picture, Molotov now is called "Vetotalitarian." His theme song is, "Accent the Negative." They Say Stalin is back at work in good spirits, and as usual, he plays his cards "close to Izvestia." As to the movies, William Powell says he is tired of playing "The Thin Man" - he wants a fat part for a change.

I think all this is awfully funny.

They say there may be two sides to the British food situation, but neither one is a side of beef. They want the UNO to take off the brass knuckles and get down to brass tacks. Got to have brass, evidently.

This man says his diary is a place to launch a thousand quips. I like the idea.

July 4, 1946

We are to celebrate the Fourth in Paris,

I like to think of it especially since the whole world believed Paris would never be capital again of anything again. We go to the Caffery reception this p.m. and to dinner with the Wildensteins afterwards.

The heat is something shocking. Records were broken yesterday. The paper says we fried in 96° heat. The French paper says 3,000 visited one swimming bath on the Seine, that we had 35° C in the shade, and the police closed their eyes when the young men jumped in the river without their plongeoirs, near the markets.

I had promised to go to tea with Mrs. Whitecotton, I tried and tried to telephone her and then went up to the Ritz just at noon in blazing heat. It was such a relief to walk into the cool Ritz. They told me that she was in the Lounge, but she was in the restaurant, so I went in there and was invited to lunch. We had a nice time. Went home to meet Dr. Monde and out to The Salpetriere. It gave me a thrill to enter the old gates and see the old catalpa trees which now are in the care of the Botanical administration of monuments. The old chestnuts and the lindens, the locusts and acacias, all trimmed and set for shape in certain places. The squares paved in the big Belgian blocks, all smoothed off by time.

Nurses, with their plain white coifs; pinned neatly around the head and hanging in the back. They look very much plainer than our girls look. They wore short-sleeved white dresses, and the aprons were a square with tapes, so it tied tightly like a man's apron. As we came or went, all the nurses rose. I felt like saying, "Ne bougez pas." But I know the doctors would not like that.

We met first in the Bureau of the Director, He was thin as a wraith and sparse as to hair, but his "favorits," or his sideburns were rather long, and though sparse, they looked hot on a hot day. He showed us in, and we met the head of Ministry of Health, a distinguished looking man, who spoke that lovely, lovely French. A delight to hear. There were two others, a historian and an engineer. Of course, we saw everything. The Head of Nursing, a powerful little woman, very earnest, as all the nurses always seem to be. She showed us classrooms, lecture rooms, demonstrations rooms, refectory, a fine room hung with a few pink and green paper garlands from the last week's fetes, the two big pianos were interesting. One was an elegant one done up in a checkerboard effect of fancy woods, with an excellent tone. It was the gift of the Queen of Rumania. The other was a huge, big, black one, a real concert grand with just a few places where it had been spoiled on the top. It was one some German general or other had and left when he fled. After a year the Americans gave it to the Salpetriere. it staggers the imagination that a general brought such a thing. We were conducted to the dining rooms, much impressed with marble top tables, service as formal as anything, in the best of the French tradition. Quite a contrast to us standing in line and toting our tray ourselves in a hot spot in the basement of New York Hospital.

There's always room here for the human being. Their gardens, their trees and plenty of time for meals.

The old women's wing was interesting. They had the old prison, and all was very well fixed. Pots of flowers on their windowsills. Their own clothes and possessions, all in one big room, down two sides. They were clean and orderly, but not in one type of clothing, not regimented at all, it seemed. They are happy, the doctor said. And sometimes they marry an old man from the old men's side. Then they go to live with the couples. No old couples ever come. He said no couples had ever applied. A good argument for marriage.

The Laundry was a new building and serves several hospitals. It was modern to the last degree. Then we had to see the Engineering side, with the piles of coal dust, the big furnaces, and so forth, modern and very well done, steam for sterilizing and so forth go on all the time.

The old insane asylum has been turned into the homes for the psychiatric cases. They are little separate houses around a court and very pretty. Will said, "Just like Jefferson had at the University of Virginia. The same detail." We went to the hospital chapel. It was enormous with a high center and four wings, all high, but not as high as the center, and all opening into the center where the altar was set. The old arrangements of Louis X IV were for different people in each separate nave. The fous the malades, the meurtrieurs, the pauvres, the old women, the old men, and the robbers - voleurs - political criminals, etc. What a sea of villainy the priest must have seen, and Communion for those all at their own railing, must have been quite a sight. All is built in the fine, old, French tradition, done by Bruant. The old man regretted that he could not show us the vases given by the Duchess of Angouleme, the daughter of Louis XVI.

We brought the two men in for dinner with us. The historian had a gunshot in the face that ruined his jaw and took all of his teeth. It passed out through the back of his neck, and he fell, and a German passed by and stabbed him in the back, breaking one of his vertebra. He lay still and later crawled to a farmhouse and was rescued. He was taken to Paris and well cared for. A new face was made for him - a good job of plastic surgery and then he was sent to Bendaye to recover. He was there for a while and then at Louvie Juzon. He did water-coloring during his two years on his back and then when he was better, he was arrested by the Germans for doing a sketch in a field, but he was released, and immediately came to Paris and served at Salpetriere for the rest of the war. He wears a lot of decorations so he must have done things in the Resistance.

The engineer has twins, a girl and a boy. The boy had finished his fourth year in medicine, but just as the war ended, he was found to have tuberculosis, so he had to leave. He is in a hospital near Grenoble.

I hope he can recover and go on with his studies.

We brought these two home to dinner with us here, and enjoyed talking with them very much, for they both have ideas about their coming to New York. I was interested in the girls' rooms. Some of them were very tidy and clean as pins, neatly decorated, The Minister was interested and kept telling me that nowadays girls, even of good families, were often poor housekeepers, not clean at all. He was so delighted with one young girl. She had it all like a pin, almost gave her the accolade. I told him that a good nurse is usually a good housekeeper, and that in the US they often marry the best of the doctors.

It was plain that he loved the old traditions of doing things, everything done as well as possible, which is hard for us Americans. We have had to be content with taking a whack at too many things to do anything impeccably well. The French want perfection. That is why they will always lead the world, I suppose. The English and the Americans can say what they wish, but they wish their idea of heaven, which is to live in Paris with all the poor from other countries excluded, for the poor French are only workers who want perfection in all things, too, especially in human dealings.

July 5, 1946

We went to the Ecole in St. Cloud, by car, today. The heat was going down and it began to rain. St. Cloud was just beginning to remove the effects of the German occupation. They have new lawns planted and flowers are in bloom, and there are lots of new works going on to clean things up the ruins from the bombings, et cetera. We drove out along the river to Argenteuil. Everywhere, men, women and children were in bathing suits, bathing in the Seine. We saw most of them on the boats of the bathing établissements. But this morning I read that three were drowned, aged 16, 18, and 21. They had plunged into the river, and they were not supported by any safety devices. It was so hot.

At Argenteuil, we met the man who had been part of the Resistance. Very sorry to find that he is in trouble with the Communists, who do not want him, and wish to do him in. We came on home and went to the Embassy and then to Wildenstein's. We loved the parties. Madame J has invited us to the opera. We were given a box. Now we must find some guests. We have three places to give away.

The article I enjoyed the most today was by Lisianne Bernhardt. She said that while "Le Grand Quatre decoup la carte du monde" meaning the Big Four cut up the map of the world, the coiffeurs are busy cutting the hair of the women the length due for the new fashions. The hair is now more important than the hat. And the hat is not right unless the hair accompanies it and must be right from each side and the front. Women's hair has always played a role in the history of love, she says. A swallow carried one of the blonde hairs of Isolde to Tristan, and it was by the long hair of Mélissande, hanging from a window, that Melissande and Peleas communicated. And then we remember the Loreléi, and the daughter of the Rhine? The women of Sparta took their hair and braided ropes which permitted their warriors to leave the ramparts.

Nowadays we couldn't do that because we have not the ramparts, neither is the hair long enough. Nowadays, one stroke of the comb gives a good coiffeur. In the old days it was otherwise. At the time of Mme. DuBarry her enemies fixed it so she would have no carriage, no dress and no coiffeur. But at six o'clock, the Duc de Richelieu sent her, in secret, the dress of his daughter, and her carriage as well, and the coiffeur Leonard. He carried the wig prepared for the daughter of the Duc. Exactly on time, Mme. DuBarry entered the throne room and that started his career. He became the coiffeur to the Queen and all the most elegant ladies.

It was Moliere who said, "We partake of the glory of our ancestors only as much as we force ourselves to resemble them."

July 6, 1946

Yesterday, Mrs. Lawrence Hill came to lunch. We had a long table talk on the politics and about the Greek Relief. She had experiences. It was quite plain she feels rather rambunctious. Mrs. MacArthur is said in reality to be the head of our Embassy, she says. We went to the Opera and had the box of the Minister of Education. It was the ballet "Lac aux Cygnes," "Coppellia," and so forth. The decor was fresh and beautiful. The decor costumes were a treat. The first had a ballet of men. Hats were tall, Turkish red fezzes. A big collar stood out of yellow shiny paper. A bright blue tunic, short sleeved, then pants a darkish old rose color, and long black stockings. Around the ankles, some rings of yellow rope. Also, a yellow sash and a long javelin in the hand. The dance was fiery and leapy and all lively and very good, Another bit, little boys with big turbans of light blue, and tunics of white, pants of bright cerise, faces dark, legs and hands held two round, yellow disks, and they danced.

The houris were adorable in old rose, long full pajamas with bloused ankles; heads covered In pale apple green; also, the face up to the eyes. Very effective.

Another costume was a shepherd's, with blue overalls, white shirts, and yellow sleeveless jackets, a large, black hat. The girls wore mustard yellow, full skirts and a tiny white apron, and a tight, bluish-green basques and white sleeves, tiny bonnets.

The creche was very simple, with an enormous ox. The ox had a wide spread of horns and the donkey with the big black ears. The three Kings were very black - one in red, one in violet, and one in yellow. Altogether, a lively decor. Our guests were Nubi and Theresa and Robert Barras. He sends his warm greetings to Jim.

Today's papers have the big news of the Bikini bathing suit. It is supposed to be the smallest one in the world. John (Tex) O'Reilly's account is funny; "Well, the French have up and done it again. This time, they've turned out the world's smallest bathing suit. I was moseying around the Rouge, yesterday, when I fell in with a big crowd moving steadily into a place. They called it a Piscine. It turned out to be a square swimming hole and they were holding a bathing beauty contest. There was a row of girls parading around in scanties, and the judges were working overtime. Every one of them, I mean the girls, was as pretty as a spotted pup under a red wagon, but then all of a sudden, a blonde named Micheline Bernardini came out in what any durn fool could see was the smallest bathing suit in the world, including West Texas. Why, folks, that suit was so small — which reminds me that in Texas there weren't any bathing suits, just no excuse for them at all. There wasn't enough water on our ranch for the cows to drink, much less, say enough to swim in. That's why heaps of people were forced into drinkin' rye whiskey, especially in the dry years."

Vincent __ reported, "How well I remember that day in 1896, when I saw a shapely calf protruding from under what I thought was a circus tent. It turned out to be a bathing suit of the period. Times have changed, judging from what I saw protruding from the Bikini model. As Einstein says, 'It's all a matter of relativity.' I am glad none of my relatives were around when I attended yesterday's display."

Well so much for that news!

July 7, 1946, Sunday

We went to see the exhibition at the Petit Palais yesterday. It was fine. Two or three excellent portraits. We went out and strolled on the Champs Elysees end had an aperitif, and we started to look for a pastry shop to get some cakes, or some bread, and found the bread but no cakes. Also, I bought a tie for Will, and we stopped to see the exhibition of modern art. Quite impressive, Home to bed early. I loved every moment. Later on, to the Dominicans to hear the opera stars. I was delighted to hear a hautbois, or some such instrument, and I loved the singing, but Dad felt It was not appropriate to church.

There was a long sermon. I saw quite a few lace veils over the girls' heads, the first since the mountains. One lady near us was in a beautiful old rose hat with feathers, and she had her little grandson. He was so dangerously thin that when we came home, we thought of him.

Then we went to see a lovely Gilbert and Sullivan show. Only a few people were present. The decor was in colors of cerise and plum, turquoise to aqua green, brown and blue. The first act in a restaurant, the canopy and the walls in muslin with pink candy stripes. The star wore purple ribbons on her blonde hair, with bunches of turquoise grapes, a white satin dress held in drapes, with the same purple gloves and shoes. Very pretty. The other star was in strontium yellow chenille dotted veiling with a basque of satin and ruches of gray, black plumes in her hair, black short mittens and black slippers. The chorus wore yellow, lavender, blue, green, scrolls on muslin dresses, and the men had coats to match. One thing at the Petit Palais was that the Germans had a museum there with enormous swastikas, etc.

July 8, 1946, Monday Paris

A beautiful editorial on July: "the month of vacations, when everyone turned the key and left for vacation. Also, the month of conspiracy and the crimes of yesterday. Seven years ago a veil of inquietude had fallen over France in 1939. The winter had passed, the writer had passed out the prizes at the Sorbonne. He looked at the happy students going away with sisters, young wives, or mothers, and he asked himself, "How long their joy could last?"

For long months, each bit of news from Germany nowadays, once more, the scar on the heart. It was written in living flesh, our alarms, the cry of the beast, the offenses to self-esteem, the menaces of those we love. July, come again. This time, thanks to God, spreads once more its promise. I hear its tones of evasion, but I cannot detach myself from the memories. They will never cease to be. History, little by little, sets them aside, gathers them up with inhuman greatness and the serenity of a fresco. The menaces there are flung on the men, the tricky promises followed by new attacks which become dates and orderly chapters, where the prize station is no more than the last breath of life. Feel keenly, the cries of the radio, the news of the night, to the titles of the daily papers, which lighted the depths of the twilight with their measured print.

History calmly transforms the trial and judgments and strong with her long experience dictates the lesson for the future. One has seen faces, unquiet for so long, regain their serenity. People reappear who have not been seen. Sad eyes reflect suddenly the clear water of joy.

July throws out its promises to these miracles. That joy must not be troubled. One does not choose, always, to forget, or to remember, and who remembers, even without demanding vigilance against hate has not thought that his memory was worth more than forgetting."

July 10, 1946, Wednesday

The Minister of Sante Publique, or Public Health, came to get us in a car. We had a warm welcome at Salpetriere. As we drove up to the old prison the iron gates were shut, and the driver honked his horn. The concierge came out and opened them. We drove into the old garden and on the benches that line the paths, in all directions, sat the elderly poor, their white heads bent over some knitting or sewing, like quiet old children. They sat in the warm evening and did busywork, at peace with the world.

We drove all the way up to the door of the building of the Nurses' School. The man with us was the Director General of Assistance Publique, that is the Public Works. They met us and I gave the two boxes of chocolates to the Directrice, and a packet of tea bags for one of the girls. I said, "Bon bons are bon, but these bon bons are not bon."

Ministre laughed, but no one else knew what I said. We had to wait for the other minister C. and his wife to arrive. We met all the attractive people. Once more, the little man with the bullet hole in his mouth, also his beautiful little wife, who is expecting a baby. And her mother, and her brother. All kind and gentle people. A charming group.

Finally, we met the two other ministers, and we all went into the big lecture room. We were shown to seats in the front row, and I sat with Count Someone on one side, and Will on the other. The lecture began. The history of Salpetriere from the start, with slides. Now and then a good little bit of entertainment. A scene from the opera, "Manon" is supposed to have taken place at Salpetriere. The scene was a screen placed before a door. When drawn back, it showed a big door with a huge lock and through the door here, bars, and a lighted space with windows of the court, and Manon well. It is still there today.

There were three young men and one girl. They were dressed in the old costumes of the time and played the love scene expertly. They belonged to an "equipe" from some theatre in Paris. Later on, two stars from the Opera Comique came on and sang the duets from the opera, "Manon", "Nous vivrons a Paris tous les deux." Perfectly beautiful. And other screen accounts with views of the old costumes, caused a riot amongst the girls — the long skirts, the high necks, and so forth. The men were even funnier than the women.

Finally, the end of that series was a little dolly dressed by the students exactly like the girls' caps and aprons, and so forth, one for each. Work uniform, dress uniform, pajamas, and the cape very cute. The program was finished by the Count, who said a few words to the girls about being dignified, etc. We all went, then, to the Refectory, and had fruit juice and cookies. They presented me with beautiful photos and even those of the dolly. The Director brought us home. We had a wonderful evening. I feel as if I could be able to nurse in Paris. No doubt I would like it at Salpetriere.

July 11, 1946, Thursday
Pasteur Valle Riradeau took us to the Rector's luncheon. Most interesting people. M. Pasteur Valle Riradeau is the grandson of Pasteur. He sat next to me. We met the Allesandres, Maggie Lescaux, and so forth. Beautiful flower arrangement of deep red roses, lavender sweet peas, and vines of light green. Later we went to tea at St. Cloud, then to Nubi's for dinner

July 12, 1946, Friday
Luncheon with the Essoberrys's (?) at the Allies' Club. She looks not only older, but brokenhearted. She is fortunate to have her boys with her. Her family suffers deeply. They are coming to lunch with us on Sunday. At the Essoberry's luncheon, a man from Sweden and a scientist with P. He was in Dachau camp for three years. He is still thin, but he was much worse. He said when he arrived, he had to push himself up against a wall in order to stand. There was a great stack of corpses lying in front of the enclosure and the German children of six

and eight played around them. It seemed unbelievable. Every day, in the paper, one is struck by the stories that are now being told. Yesterday, it was an entire family, father, mother and daughter of twenty-one, all interned in Ravensbruck, where they died, and a service was held in memory of them at the Israelite Synagogue. The mother, born Dorothea Schwartz, the husband, Something Cohen. Also, the death of a young man, very suddenly, of appendicitis. He spent two years in Dachau. He was twenty-three years old.

July 14, 1946, Sunday

The Esoberry's came to lunch with us, with their son, Pierre. He is a good, big, good-looking, clever boy,' at the Ecole Normale. She told me one funny bit about a German. The name was von Bouliers. The family was French. Under Louis XIV, they were driven out and went to Germany, and now he wanted to renew his French citizenship, and had already received his permission from Hitler. His desire was to bring good, strong, virile, German blood into the weak French nation, and to improve the stock, as his stock had been improved. Their friend, on Friday, said that he and other intelligentsia were thrown into a space with 500 others, all filled with bugs and lice and fleas. They had no water, no soap, no sanitary devices. They decided, at least, to use their brains, so everyone was told he must clear himself of all vermin. Kill them by hand. After that, each one was examined by his fellows constantly. If a new one came, they told him to clean himself of his bugs first, and no one would touch him until he had freed himself. They never had any form of epidemic in that enclosure while typhus and so forth raged every place else.

Certain of the women did extremely well. One woman in a women's camp, started competitions in sewing and drawing, and, of all things, cooking. At first, if a packet arrived, each one grabbed, ate it up, gorged herself, became ill and so forth. After this, the women got together. They took the chocolate and cooked it up in cakes and so forth; they shared with all of the camp. Gradually, it grew to be a contest in invention and the ideas flowed. The women made out much better than the men. They wrote stories for each other, they put on plays, they knitted and sewed amusing things, they made fete days. I was most interested. I said, how in the world did they cook? She said they all had a little pan and one tiny place to cook. Evidently, they planned for days in order to do it at a special time.

She showed me pictures of her father's home. It was evidently very large and was nothing but one big chimney in the picture. Her entire family were requisitioned, as they were doctors. Even her sisters and brothers—in-law served the Germans in the Underground Hospital in Berlin, until the Americans freed them. We went to see Yvonne Printemps in "Aupres de ma Blonde" How musty, dusty, and weak it is compared to the others we have seen.

July 16, 1946, Tuesday

Chambriun came to dinner. He told of his great misery. About France. About how he suffered, and so forth. We tried to pour it on that France is great. I think he felt a little better, He said, all that saved his sanity was laughing at themselves. Also, they began to play tricks on the Germans. At first, they were routed at six o'clock in the morning for exercises. Then they began getting all mixed up and running into one another and pretending to misunderstand, and so forth, and such chaos that they finally plotted ahead. Finally, the Germans stopped the exercises and began to drill singing. So they sang insulting songs in French about the Germans. Finally, the Germans caught on to some of it and they even quit the singing. So they were left alone. They had football, tennis, and so forth, toward the end, but the two first years were torture. They received packages from the Red Cross, which they cooked for themselves, and when they could. They built a fireplace and the Russians who went out as slaves, brought in wood, so they would have quite good meals and gave their turnip soup to the Russians in exchange for wood. They slept out-of-doors in the summer, and all had fleas, and so forth. They put on plays. He rose and acted in some of them. It was a camp full of talent and all refused to do slave labor, except the Russians. His suit is like chiffon. We must send him some flannels.

We had lunch with the Minister of Uruguay. Darling people. We went to a Spanish restaurant. They told about the "pocket battleship" Admiral Graf Spee. How it came into Montevideo looking so huge and bristling with guns. The tiny place ordered them to leave, and a few boats from the Government, or there would be no city left. But they left like sheep. As they steamed out of the harbor there were millions of people watching. The Argentine ships appeared and circled around. No one knew what it was, and then they saw the crew jump off and swim toward the Argentine ship. They all climbed aboard, and it steamed away with them. Suddenly a big explosion took place, and the Graf Spee went down. Everyone thought the English had shot it down, until later on, they found out the Germans had sunk it themselves.

July 19, 1946
We had our dinner last night. I wore my black taffeta with white earrings. Will had a very little car. After getting the dress all beautifully pressed, I had to ruin the skirt in the car. It was so mussed up, However, no doubt no one knew it but me. We arrived at the club, more or less weighed down. The Walmsleys brought cigarettes and whiskey, and Dad had them in the valise. I had a box of chocolates. Jane sent them. And the place cards and menus. Mr. Aime Lerois came to lunch and helped me to write up all the names properly.

Being "ancien ambassadeur" we were glad to be able to rest all of that on his willing head. He also typed Dad's talk. He has been a friend indeed. The dinner came off very nicely. The Ambassador told me he had had to give a cocktail party to the visiting editors and the Duke of Windsor had called and stayed on for the party. He was to leave for a vacation but stayed for dinner. Mrs. Caffery is very "gentile" We both like her ever so much. Nubi and Teresa were such a help. The Schneiders were a real prize. In fact, all in all, it was a treat and I'm sure the others enjoyed it as well as ourselves.

We arrived beforehand to see that all was in place. The table was looking very nice, but there were no flowers. The room for the cocktails was full of elderly French people, mostly women, very much made up, with feather boas, and so forth. They had had a tea party. Eight p.m. was nothing to them. We finally asked the maitre d'hotel to tell them to go. Nothing doing. They got awfully curious and insisted on looking at our table and, thank goodness, it didn't look much, By the time the florists arrived, they had begun to go, and just as Mr. and Mrs. Dawes walked in, the last of them left.

The boys began to place the chairs against the wall and open up the windows and air out the smoke, and they hastily cleared up the buffet, brought in a big basket of glasses, and soon had our party in some sort of shape. We ordered the flowers in the Tri-Couleur, red, white, and blue, and there was a blaze of light under the electric chandelier. I could have liked it more if the beautiful crystal had been cleaned, but the dinner was excellent end the waiters all very good indeed.

Will gave a toast. He referred to a speech he heard. The nicest bit was the way he ended it. "Je leve mon verre, etc... Vive Les Etats Unis! Vive La France." The Minister of Education then rose, and he referred to the kind remarks Will had made on the art exhibitions which came under his personal direction. Then he disagreed with a speech that Will had referred to, that France was a tiny chick between two great eagle powers, etc. He ended, Vive les Etats Unis, Vive La France. The Ambassador did not wish to speak, so that ended the toasts. They wanted to know the speech that Will had quoted from, and he said it was one by Pierre __. Then he added that, no doubt, it was indiscreet. It must have been the champagne that made him indiscreet. I was afraid he meant what he said, but it was his way of settling all their minds, for everyone was very curious.

14

July 1946 - London

Editor's Note: In 1987, in celebration of Dr. Johnson's 278's birthday, Phyllis Rowell published her account of caretaking Dr. Johnson's house during the war years. Although there are some inconsistencies, Chloe's account dovetails with that of Mrs. Rowell and was certainly noted much closer in time to the actual events.

July 20, 1946, Sunday
We came to London by plane and landed about noon. The drive into Duke's was very interesting.

July 24, 1946
We went to the House of Commons, and there was just one place. I said I would like to go to the House of Lords to see Montgomery take his bow. Soon there was a Sergeant to lead me. I went along past people having... (page missing)
...I was interested in the costume of one who led in the new Lords. It was thick and stiff with golden embroidery with coats of arms, crouching lions, unicorns, rampant lions on red, and then a beautiful gold harp on a field of blue. His thin, little legs in long black silk stockings

and patent leather pumps with large silver buckles — solid silver, I'm sure, and fine in the English style... (page missing)

...full of gold and perfectly beautiful. In the House of Lords, they let me stand with a group. Finally, we got seats. I missed the speeches, but I saw the men and their sponsors, with all their scarlet robes. The Lord Chancellor, when he entered, with the elderly page bearing his long train, the other going before holding up the huge, gold mace. His wig must have been hot.

Now and then he took off the top of it and lifted It. The other two in wigs had their backs to me and the little queues and the curls looked very odd. Lord Pembroke read a long report on taxes. No more taxes on hair-waving, he said. He didn't care, as he is bald, but he was interested in the next item. It was that there is to be no more tax on wigs.

Will & Chloe were friends with Viscount Montgomery. This photo was taken during a later meeting, probably in the 1950's
Russell Family Archive

Before we go on with that I must talk about Montgomery, who came in and wearing all his robes, and was made an Earl.

July 26, 1946

Will and I walked through the melancholy ruins of the Temple and went along what is left of Pater Noster Row. We wandered about in and out of the old familiar places. We stood and gazed into wild growth clustering around some rusty bits of iron that were lying in a sort of excavation that was once the basement of Simpsons-in-Cheapside. We yearned over the memory of the Fish Ordinary we once enjoyed in that excellent restaurant. We remembered the colossal cheese whose weight we were supposed to guess. What a cheese! That memory was especially painful because we have been learning what it is like to be rationed and England without cheddar cheese is hardly England.

Searching for some familiar thing in the ruins we thought we could detect the outlines of a rusty Chef's stove amidst the welter, but nothing else was left to recall the good life of the bye-gone days.

Wandering on, we finally came to the entrance to Gough Square, so we followed the narrow passage hoping to see Dr. Johnson's house, but fearful of finding more wreckage.

The house was standing quite intact, clean, and tidy and obviously cared-for. Blackened ruins stretched away in all directions as far as the Thames. The caretaker's cottage still snuggled up against the big building toward Fleet Street and the door opened just then. A neat, dark-eyed woman with graying hair came out. Did we want to see the house? If so, then too bad, but no visitors were being admitted because of reparations after the Blitz.

We wanted to know where she had been during that awful time.

"Right here all the time"

Then she began to tell us about what she had done; one small, frail woman, quite alone!

Her name is Mrs. Rowell and she told about the worst night. It was December twenty-fourth. The weather had turned extremely cold. The Thames froze, the tide was out, the Locks had been stuck and there was a fight on to save the Lock-gates. Water pressure was down to nothing, and the water froze in the hoses. That night the Nazis chose to give London a saturation bombing.

She tried to sit quietly in her shelter but found she couldn't do it. She mounted the roof of Dr. Johnson's house carrying a stirrup-pump and pails of water.

Great showers of burning embers were pouring down from all sides. Searchlights were whirling back and forth over-head. Bombs were crashing and a sea of flames and smoke billowed over all the sky. Just then a few men ran into the square. They were volunteer firemen. As they crossed the square a tall building collapsed and fell on them. She was going to drop everything and go to them when others came running and began to dig amongst the ruins.

She continued pumping and fetching buckets of water for now the roof was smoldering. Alone amidst such sights of destruction from her perch, she saw the bodies of the three volunteers brought out; she saw firemen come wearily into the square dragging their trucks. A mere tiny trickle came from the hoses – and even that froze as it fell.

She kept on doing what she blindly found before her, carrying water from her tiny kitchen, and pumping it over the roof.

Finally, she felt it was safe to quit. As far as she could see, fires were raging unchecked.

She came down to her little house and built a fire on the hearth. All gas and electric lights were gone, so she stuck candles in some bottles and proceeded to make tea.

Then she went out and called in the Volunteers.

They came in out of the freezing dawn. She said they were a most pitiful sight. Aside of their helmets they were wearing their own civilian clothes, which were in a dreadful state; soaking wet, covered with lime and mud and their shoes a sodden mess.

The men were grateful for the warmth, and she kept tea going constantly as one after another, they continued to come for hours on end to rest for a moment, then back at the hopeless task.

During the following days, Mrs. Rowell went to the Red Cross and begged for woolen clothes for the volunteer firemen. She was able to get some sea-boot socks, great, long white wool socks. Then she found someone to issue rubber boots, then gloves. She begged for waterproof garments of any kind. The different services were all beautifully cared for, with full uniforms, but the poor Volunteers had to use their own clothes and their work was of the hardest. Her personal efforts yielded many benefits. Each time she asked, something was forthcoming, and she passed it on at once to the Volunteers.

The Red Cross gave her powdered milk and tea and biscuits and every night, all night, her hearth-fire was bright and hot tea was always on the hob.

Volunteer firemen came in as if to a Club. Night after night she was always ready for them with a warm welcome.

One night, during a particularly awful raid, many men she had never seen before came. One lad opened the door. He glanced around the room crowded with Volunteers sitting everywhere. On the floor, on tables. In the windows deep embrasures were set many beer bottles with lighted candles. Everybody was sipping hot tea. The newcomer pulled off his helmet and pretended to stagger.

"Blimey" he shouted, "It looks like a bloomin' Christmas tree!" When the laugh died down, he looked at Mrs. Rowell and said quietly,

"It's hard to say which is brighter; out there (waving at the blazing ruins) or in here!"

Her son-in-law was one of the Volunteers. One night he came in with his usual crowd. They were particularly tired and late; she enquired why.

It seemed that after one bad crash, they were working to get everybody out and at last it seemed all were accounted for. They were leaving when they heard a kitten mewing. They still felt fairly peppy, so one of the chaps said,

"What say Lads – do we try to get kitty?"

Some said yes, others no and the ayes had it, so they began to dig. After a while the sound ceased so they called,

"Here kitty, kitty," A woman's voice answered them.

"It isn't a kitty," the voice said, "it's a baby. I have it in my arms, but a beam is lying on my legs so I can't move."

The men began to shine their torches in the direction of the voice.

"Shut your eyes" they said, "we are shining very strong torches your way."

"Never mind," came the voice gently, "It doesn't matter because I am blind."

They came to her at last and saved both the woman and the baby.

Another night Mrs. Rowell told us about was late in the war when the flying bombs were crashing before their sound could warn people to take shelter. The son-in-law came in Saturday afternoon and said he intended to have an afternoon of rest. Just then a flying bomb crashed in the near vicinity. He grabbed helmet, mask and axe and ran out towards Fleet Street.

Some hours later he came back very tired and stood out-side the door. Mrs. Rowell opened the door for him, but he just stood there. He was muddy and dripping.

"Come on in Son," she said.

"Oh, I just can't," he said, "I just can't"

"Why, what's the matter?"

"Oh, it was so awful," he said. "It struck in Shaftsbury Avenue – and there's a hole big enough to drive a bus into, just in front of the Post Office. The blast blew a big safe down through the floor. It crashed through the floor and was hanging half-way through to the basement. We had to lift it because there were five girls in the basement shelter. It was a tricky business, lifting it."

When it was lifted, they went down to rescue the girls and found them all lying dead from shock, their hair standing up still on their heads and all a gray color.

"Those were his very words," said Mrs. Rowell. "I just said – drop your clothes where you are, Son. They can never be any use anymore. I'll run a hot bath for you, and you come inside in your birthday-suit and get straight into the tub.

"He did," she said, "and after that I gave him lunch, but it was days before he could smile again."

By this time, we all felt such bonds of sympathy that we could hardly part, so she invited us to come in and look through the precious house and see the beams on the top floor where the fire had been extinguished by her efforts. Then we were shown rolls of carpet, the gift of the American branch of the Pilgrim Society. Then we went downstairs and learned the secret of Dr. Johnson's front-door lock. We looked out into Gough Square at the ruins that had fallen on the three men and off into the blue haze above the Thames. It was a sudden feeling that here amongst the English, the world's greatest appreciators – of Art – of Literature – of Drama – on and on. Many things would be lost to the world but for the appreciation of the English – especially Shakespeare and Shaw and surely Dr. Johnson. These people fought to save the relics of such a worthy person. What worthy people are these!

We said good-bye to the smiling little lady so cool and steady no Blitz could shake her. She is a person I will never forget.

July 27, 1946

Came to Dublin yesterday. Agreeable trip. We had so much to eat — we ate all day long. Early breakfast, tea and toast in our room at Duke's. On the train, breakfast, bacon and sausages and coffee, about nine. A lunch of soup and lamb, and so forth, at 11:30. Tea on the Irish boat: a mutton chop, and fried potatoes, and tea, at about 5:30. Dinner here at 8:30. Lamb, peas, trifle, and the richest of whipped cream. Never cold or uncomfortable once the whole day.

All around us, poor people held paper suitcases so loaded down that they could hardly lift them. What could be so heavy? Books is all I can think of, but we think it was food; hams, bacons, and so forth, or else just bottles of drink. Many English people, so we were ashamed to take any privileges. They seem grabby, rude and not to look ahead and have no manners. I'm sure England, without the aristocrats, would be a bad place to live.

Ireland is pretty, but full of little, uncared-for, fat children. We saw many tiny little girls, pretty as angels, all dirty and in rags; out running in the streets. And little boys were yelling and playing in the streets until midnight. I feel like a Scotch Presbyterian here. I want to whip the people and say, "Go home and clean up your children." However, there is a peaceful air about everything.

The only people who would be truly unhappy here would be my family. My mother would hate every stick and stone of it and be outraged to see the dirty children. My father would not like all that food and drink and whipped cream, and to see so many dirty people standing around begging. As for me, I feel as if I lived here, at worst I would not be allowed to like my window. An old wrought iron curtain rod tied with dusty cream-colored, lacquer red, soft pink, dull blue, and dull green ribbons; two crystal candle sticks with two black gloves sticking up on top. I prefer my own way: clean and neat and orderly. I feel there is no freedom here. It seemed like my idea of Russia. Everyone has to live like a rabbit.

15

April 1953 - Hail Women of Rio

Editor's Introduction: Based on events and persons named, it is probable that this trip took place in 1953, shortly before Will retired from Teacher's College and joined a precursor of the CIA. Over the course of the trip, Chloe was privileged to meet all the major figures of the Brazilian feminist movement. Although she presents an idealized portrait of Rio, her emphasis on diversity and women's rights is in alignment with the forward-thinking orientation of Teacher's College.

This year a special honor came to Teachers College and to my husband. He was invited to go to Rio to give a series of lectures. He was asked to bring me, and all expenses were to be paid by the Brazilians. They say they do not like the State Department to choose the people they invite; they prefer to choose for themselves. So, we went as guests of the Instituto Brazilio-Estados Unidos.

The invitation came as a surprise and when we decided to accept, we felt we were doing something strange. We had travelled often to

Europe and out to China and Japan, but of the great stretches below the Equator, we knew almost nothing.

We planned our 66 lbs. of luggage so as to have clothes for cold weather; "Remember," said our friends "down there it is winter." Then on April 23rd we drove to through Harlem and over the Triboro Bridge to Idlewild Airport.

It was a balmy day, and all Harlem was basking in the sunshine. Men were wearing soft felt slouch hats. We never saw a man wearing a hat again until we came home. I make one exception, the men who collect the garbage and trash in Rio, have big baskets to carry it to the big Sanitation trucks. They carry them on their heads; so to make the scalp more comfortable they put two or three old felt hats in a stack on their heads and rest the basket on that cushion.

The women in Harlem were relaxing; they strolled up and down, some wearing fur coats. They chewed gum or smoked cigarettes. There were lines waiting to get into the moving-picture theater. Each side of the door stood big posters showing a beautiful actress with dark flowing curls, she was struggling with a muscular man whose face was distorted with fury, her dress was red. The posters blared

Based on the date & image, the poster Chloe saw may have been for this film
www.imdb.com/title/tt0046457/

in big print: "Violent! Shocking! Brutal!" and all the world flocked to be entertained by that.

We passed the A&P Supermarket. Through acres of plate-glass we could see neat packages ranged along shelves; people pushing wire baskets on wheels crammed with the packaged articles done up in cellophane and paper wrappings; clean enough and beautiful enough, I hope, to be suitable for people living many to a room, as I am told they often do. We were leaving all this, and I seemed to be seeing it for the first time as I tried to imagine what would greet our eyes waking in Rio, half a world away.

The next morning, our airplane was coasting down over a smooth harbor. Great rocks were pushing up from the water in prehistoric-looking shapes. We were flying through a sort of dream-world, all blue sky, golden sun and shining water, dotted with these strange great shapes of mountains. It is all very well to describe how the earth's surface cooled, the lava flowed away, and these granite piles remained; their outlines are marks in a sea-scape where man is definitely a Pygmy – and this is Rio de Janeiro – a new world to be described.

Postcard from Russell family archives

As our Plane coasted in, dwarfed by the greatness of the harbor, we saw on the highest of the rocks, the tremendous figure of Christ – the Corcovado. His arms are raised, open wide in a gesture of welcome and blessing. He seems to be saying, "enter and sup with me, welcome stranger!" He sets a seal upon this place; here one finds gentle people and a warm welcome.

The Airport is an experience, not a building! It is a design for happy landings. The structure rests on pillars and between them cool breezes blow. That was important to us, because for us it seemed warm weather. There were glass louvers, spotless stone floors and walls also of stone; the counters for luggage were low. There was a large parking lot, and our friends were there to meet us.

Then began a tour of infinite variety. We drove along the shore and passed the new University. I began to think this must be Paradise for any student. Spaciousness, simple and grand – the first floor supported on a forest of tall columns, open on all sides to form a huge gathering place, in shelter from sun and rain. A good arrangement, no campus to cross; walk up stairs to classrooms; stone benches for a rest and smoke and columns, columns, columns! Space-limited New York could appreciate such an arrangement. I wish we might have it here.

As we drove along, we passed some tall, old red-brick buildings. Someone said they look like Germany; then there were stretches where we said, "How much this is like Paris." Later on, we would say, "Look how much this is like London". Later still, Italy and so on... It seems that Rio is made up of big population groups, like New York. The main difference seems to be that our foreign elements fit into our city as they find it – in Rio, they give their civilization to the city.

Finally, we progressed into the suburbs with names like the notes of a scale played on a harp – Copacabana – Botafogo – Ipanema – Gavea.

Now we ran along a shore of soft white sand, swept and beaten by the great curling waves of the Atlantic. Running alongside the highway, we saw for the first time, that striking specialty; sidewalks made of tiny black and white stones, laid in a mosaic pattern sometimes representing waves, sometimes geometric designs – always a work of art.

Postcard from Russell Family Archives

They are laid lavishly throughout the city, apparently the workmen are born knowing how to make them. I never set foot on one or crossed one without feeling a sort of heart-throb and thinking, "This is something ancient, to be treasured. A symbol of an older civilization of a high order."

Day after day from my hotel window, I watched the waves wash in and retreat. Never a bit of paper or refuse of any kind. At first, I marveled at the dignity and good manners of the people, then later my heart began to bleed – what makes our beaches so untidy? Why do we leave papers, beer-cans, Coca-Cola bottles and orange skins all around? For nineteen days it was spread before me like a giant book from my hotel window, there it was – what a really grown-up, responsible people can do.

Those people seemed to be dignified first of all; second, they seemed to be polite. They took their places in queues as if by right and I never saw a one break out of line. The water system was being changed, so for a few hours in the mornings the water would be turned off to accommodate the workmen. People would take bottles and pitchers and go down to the sidewalk where carts would be drawn up, doling out water from big tanks. The apartment-house dwellers would drop into line to get the water they needed; no one shoved ahead or showed the slightest anger with the inconvenience.

Our hotel was modern and when we arrived, I expressed my delight to see a wide stone terrace invitingly arranged with tables and chairs for one to observe the sea, the beach, the boulevard and sidewalk life while having refreshments. "That is where I shall spend hours" I said, "I love a sidewalk Café." Before I go further, I as well add that I never sat there for a single moment. I forgot all about it, there were so many other fascinating things to do.

The first night we tried to find the Southern Cross, but a rainstorm blew up. Each evening after that we searched the sky and each time it clouded over so it wasn't until much later when we reached Santiago in Chile that we saw the spectacular Southern Cross. It was worth the waiting for that one cold evening; it was so brilliant.

Searching the sky as we did, we found the Big Dipper and it was lying strangely along the horizon. The moon was full while we were there, and it was sailing away up – and as for the sun – the sunlight wasn't right, and we never got used to sunsets in the north.

At the back of our hotel one of the granite hills rose up steeply. It was dotted to the top with little homes and gardens. I asked about it.

"Oh, those are our slums," said my friend, we are going to do away with that and build a housing development."

"But you have miles and miles of the most modern skyscrapers. You have all manner of housing developments. Why not leave this neat orderly bit of human living. Everything is so clean and swept—not a speck of dust out of place! There seems to be a tiny garden, a banana tree and a little cozy wattle hut. Wouldn't it, be a good idea to preserve this bit of life so near to Mother earth? Surely everybody doesn't want to live in a skyscraper."

"You surprise me" said my friend, "In New York you have nothing like this in Harlem."

"Ah Harlem---" I sighed. "I prefer to think about your beaches."

The mixture of races in Rio is more like New York than any other great city. They too have large groups of French, Italian, German, Negro, Japanese and North American as well as their own Indian and Brazilian. We visited schools and hospitals and churches as well as the Press Club, the Libraries and other places where we saw people at work and at play; there was no evidence of discrimination of any kind.

We were taken to the races as guests of a member of the exclusive Jockey Club. There we saw a tall well-dressed man sitting in a group of smartly dressed men and women. He was the only negro in that group, and someone pointed him out, as the owner of one of the fine horses winning a race. Many other obviously well thought-of people were moving about in their well-mannered way, negroes thoroughly at home.

We visited an exclusive school. The pupils are accepted only after competition, scholarship tests and personality checks. We saw girls from all walks of life. Uniforms are required, white socks and blouses and a navy-blue jumper dress with a pleated skirt. Everyone wore impeccable white, and the uniforms were most becoming. Some of the children can't afford them but that, is no problem because there are also girls who request the privilege of paying for some of the others.

That was an indication of the spirit of the school. There were rich and poor; pretty and not so pretty; all races and types and all seemed to share certain traits; they were surprisingly dignified, kind, bright, and polite.

The young woman who took us to visit the school was a lovely looking person who had taken her degree at our college, Teacher's College. Her name is Arici Freire – the name so odd and beautiful that I asked about it.

"It is ancient Indian" she said, "it means Moon-Flower"

They say there is nothing in a name, but when I knew that, both the name and the bearer seemed enhanced. I remarked to the Principal that the students spoke a fluent, easy English. "Do they all speak it at home?" I asked.

"Oh no indeed" Then he propounded to me, his system for the

practice of languages; he makes them sing the popular songs. Then he called on some classes to sing for us and we felt right at home with girls' voices singing "On Top of Old Smokey"! I shut my eyes and thought of my granddaughters.

At recreation time they filled the halls with gay chatter; then the bells rang, and they began to disappear into doorways. I saw them wave a hand and smile and say to their friend, something that sounded like, "Tay-ja!" Arici said, "They are saying "be seeing you." How much more like home can you get?

All day long as long as daylight lasted there were people on the beach. Beginning about 7 am men in swimming trunks began to appear along the beach, apparently the same men each day. They would emerge from the hotels and apartment houses, cross the street and go for a swim. From our window we watch them plunge through the great, green wheel of the surf, then swim out beyond the breakers, turn and come back coasting on a wave. Soon women would begin to follow. They were usually quite sun-tanned and tall and long-legged, wearing a Bikini suit. We could guess their nationality to be Scandinavian, German, or North American because of their athletic appearance and way of striding. About 8:30 they would have disappeared, and men and boys would be seen coming from the side streets for their swim, later they would be gone and about 9 o'clock, out would come the family life. Papa bearing a huge umbrella, Mama with the little ones, Nurse with the sand buckets, the baby carriages and the bigger children. A sort of family life would spread out in brilliant colors of beach blankets, umbrellas, bathing-suits, people sun-bathing and children with big hats busy digging. Around noon, all this would disappear and from then the beach would be taken over by the footballers. From noon until dark games of soccer would be set up all along the miles and miles of sand and go on without interruption. It seems that then the beach belongs to the men and boys and to their national sport, soccer. It is as if we abandoned miles of New York waterfront, every day, for the men and boys to play baseball.

The first groups would bring umpires, goal posts, wear uniforms, have nets, etc. Others just had a ball. As far as the eye could see, games would be in progress. We never ceased to marvel at the agility and long-windedness of the players; they would kick the ball backwards sending it just where they wanted. They butted it with the head, stopped it with the foot, turned it and sent it with the instep – and all done barefoot. I met one man who had been the most famous of the footballers. I asked him if it wasn't harmful to the bones of the feet to play bare footed.

"Oh no" he said, "I've been playing barefooted since I was three years old."

After a short time watching the games from our window, we would know the players and take sides. This was better than a sidewalk café.

At intervals another slice of life would take over the beach. There used to be big fishing fleets in Brazil, but during the war all small craft were discontinued, and they have not yet permission to go out of the harbor to fish, so they fish now along the beach. The boats go out with two men rowing and one man standing. He would pay out a large net coiled in the bottom of the boat as they went. Out beyond the surf,

Postcard from Russell Family Archives

in calm water the weighted net would be lowered, and the two rowers would take a rope and swim in to the shore where eager men and boys would form lines and tug the net in. They would drag and drag until at last the fish would be piled up on the sand. The people who helped to pull in the net would get their share, some housewives would buy, and big flat baskets piled with fish would be carried back through the streets on the heads of men to homes or markets. Then the beach would go back to sunning or soccer.

Perhaps this paints too relaxed and easy a life. The people are hardy and seem to work for pleasure just as hard as they play. Mornings they are hammering on the myriads of new buildings by seven; crowded buses were tearing into the city, streetcars with people hanging at all sorts of precarious angles would go past. The streets are jammed with all manner of workers, no time off, no siesta in Rio! Then the moment their work is done, off they go to the hill to work in the garden or to the beach to play soccer. It being fall, it grows dark at about 6 o'clock and leaves blow along the streets.

Rio is somewhat like New York in being limited in width. We have the Hudson and East Rivers, they have the steep, unyielding granite mountains. The only really free access to the rest of the country is by plane, for roads are only through the passes, one reason for the development of their airfields and ports to such greatness.

The city is much like Wall Street of a Sunday, Saturday or holiday. Then it seems that the entire population must be spending the day on the beaches, however there is a gigantic football stadium seating more than 200,000. The racing stands are crammed, but no waiting lines as the Cinema. There was the same film we had seen drawing crowds in Harlem – but here people swept past without so much as a glance at the dark-haired actress in the red dress.

We weren't in Rio long before we began to notice that there exists a sort of protective custody over old things and at the same time everything modern does have the warmest reception of any place I've seen. They guard the old with all their hearts and then show all enthusiasm possible for the glass houses and towering edifices of the new age. An example of what I mean is right on the big boulevard that runs along the sea. It has been reclaimed from the sea and is filled in land for long stretches at one spot there is a great white modern hotel. On the cliff above it sits a tiny chapel, Our Lady of Glory they call it or The Gloria.

It is a quaintly beautiful little Chapel with a wainscoting throughout of delft tiles representing the coming of the early discoverers, with plumed hats in hand bowing to the Indians with their head-dresses. I wanted to go all around and follow the story in the tiles, but a wedding ceremony was in progress, and we couldn't.

The Madonna of the Gloria does not hold the infant in her arms; her hands are joined as in prayer and a cherubim cluster above around her feet where she stands on the crescent moon. For my most cherished souvenir I brought back an antique figure of Gloria. A friend said he thought I had chosen something that no country outside Brazil had made. We found that out to be true. Primitive artists made them for every home in the earliest days.

Nowadays The Gloria sits above the busy boulevard, above the great modern hotel and there the young come and go for their wedding day.

Social services show the same spirit. Portuguese civilization was essentially a matriarchy. The mother or the grandmother was responsible not only for the health services and the nursing but also the monetary transactions, the animal husbandry, the weaving and lacemaking, the household and the slaves. The custom was to send the young girls to Europe to be educated so when they married, they could read, write and figure, speak several languages, know the most subtle cooking, how to care for the sick, how to treat wounds, and on and on. In addition, the education of the women and the children was her responsibility. The results are impressive. I have seen the weaving, and the laces made on the plantations from the designs of some grandmothers. We were regaled everywhere with food that was made from the old recipes gathered if not invented by past generations of women.

One American said to me "Just think! There are no organized charities in Brazil!" He spoke as if he were airing a scandal. I almost asked him if he had heard the scandal being aired about our highly organized charities that have become so top heavy and bureaucratized that the office staff receive most of the proceeds from almost any big benefit we work to sell tickets for - to our disappointment.

In Rio their charities are as old as the country. It may seem at first as if little is needed, but there are improvements going on all the time. One day I was invited to attend the opening of a new wing at the mother's clinic. It is simply called Pro Matre or For Mother.

We were greeted at the door by Jeronima Mesquita. Her friends told me that she is a moving spirit in all the good works of the city. She it was who came to New York about 30 years ago to meet and confer with Mrs. Valentine Macy, the wife of our trustee. Girl Scouts were just starting, and Mrs. Macy was a prime mover. Jeronima went to Camp Editha Macy and imbibed the things she took home to Rio to start the Girl Scout movement there. I was interested to meet some of her first groups and also the children of the first ones. This is just one of her accomplishments.

Meeting Dona Jeronima was a privilege. She is not young anymore and she told me that in the course of her life the most striking memory is seeing her father freeing his slaves. At the time she was a small girl of five or so. Slavery ceased in Brazil about 10 years later than the US and her father was ahead of his time in doing it of his own choice. The prodigious importance of his act at that time seems to be reflected in her sharp memory of it.

The work of Pro Matre began small many years ago and has been expanding ever since. The service is much like ours at New York Hospital; the mothers come in early in their pregnancy and after that report regularly. When their time is up their service becomes different from ours. In the US the mother has to leave the hospital after four or five days and go home. The Brazilian system is quite a departure. To begin with when the mother comes in, she brings the smaller children with her from her family. They are fed and cared for until she is entirely ready to go home. It doesn't matter if it takes days or weeks or months or a year!

The women who direct and finance this worthy project are busy mothers of families themselves. They are also highly educated and speak English as well as I do, fluent French and of course Spanish and Portuguese. They give their time faithfully as they say, "in days and out days". They're so used to taking initiative that if they see some need, they are likely to found an Institute to care for that need. Individual initiative works all manner of miracles. For instance, at a reception friends introduced a tall, dark eyed woman of commanding presence. She had glowing eyes and white hair brushed smoothly back. "She is responsible for eradicating leprosy here", said my friends. We intended to visit her laboratories but did not have time.

Our friend Ignez Barros-Bareta Araujo had occasion to deal with refugees who flooded Rio with the coming of the Fascist and Nazi regimes. She found they could not become citizens; not being citizens they could not get a job - or charity - or medical attention. The government wanted no piece of them. They had enough to think of with submarines, fishing boats and myriads of other wartime troubles, so she decided to act. She came up to Washington where my husband was hard at it trying to help Uncle Sam with the same immense problem. We had millions of aliens to turn into citizens. She appealed to him and he gave her all of his material. She went back in established - with her own funds - a foundation to do the work. She ran it herself for some time, but now she had turned it over to the government and has retired from directing it. There is the resulting interest that due to her efforts the public was aroused to the need and from that had sprung a real place for refugees in Brazil.

The poor are never forgotten in Rio. It has been said that the Ten-Cent-Store is the poor man's club in the USA. That paradise where a few pennies will buy almost anything and where the poorest person may be warm and have all that the little match girl had in her visions - without burning a match. In Rio we wandered in the markets feeling that same way; a very few pennies seemed to buy so much, and such a wealth of fruit and melons and vegetables could only be imagined in a dream. Melons about two feet long and another two feet around. Mangoes really a dime a dozen and the other fruits so beautiful and exotic. Ignez kept bringing them to us and giving their names and home province. "Pernambuco", she would say or some other place. I find I can't remember any names, but I recall the flavors. Even the bananas deserve a booklet. Every size and color and myriad of uses. One is about 18 inches long and made into flour cooked into soups and other things I never used dreamed of using the banana for! Other kinds of for eating but none seemed like ours.

As I've said, they never forget the poor; there are small fruits and other things of different kinds for cheaper prices. Even the eggs! I'm so used to our products all one size and all one price that I was entranced. They have a sort of hunk of something like the root of a tree. It is a sort of material that is made into flour and sliced thin like a sort of a potato chip and good. We had some frequently.

I have made no mention of the flowers for that way lies madness... just the foliage is a gardens woman's dream and for the orchids - and roses are so really roses!

Their plant preservation is a tremendous affair. Brazil was named for a tree that startled the first settlers because when the bark is stripped back it shows a brilliant blazing red and Brazil means burner.

The whole country is filled with the most fabulous plants and trees. It thrilled me to visit the Botanical Gardens. They were established by King John about the year 1815. He hoped to preserve the amazing rare and sturdy plants growing in that new world. So it is set up in a Royal way; everything in perfect order shells of tiniest plants in flats, then a bigger lot and then they are set out in tiny pots, then larger and larger and finally the tree or plant is pointed out growing tall an old in the garden. There is a row of palms from the first planted by King John.

There is the Jaracanda tree, so much used in the finest furniture. Then the Travelers tree which is so valuable to the dry countries. You stab it with a knife, and it obliges with spouting a stream of cool water. It is very good - I know because I tasted it when the curator asked me to.

One tree we were shown was most well organized. It grows its own vine for decoration. It is a tall tree, and the foliage grows away high; and then about 2 feet from the roots a vine emerges and twines itself up to the trunk drooping Flowers of a lovely pink along the way. The flowers are like five pink seashells clustered around a tiny crown.

Perhaps best known of the plants is the Victoria Regia - a water Lily with a leaf 4 feet across. It is so thick it looks as if it were made of tin and the underlining is a Christmas red. To believe it one must see it.

Along the Amazon there is a tree that has seeds that float in a little white boat. They float for thousands of miles and come to land and then unload their seeds.

There is a poem about Rio: There was an Angel who went out to fly around the world and gather up a sample of the best thing from each country. The poem goes that when she arrived at Rio her apron slipped, and all the best things fell down on Rio. I'm sure the story must be true.

Dona Jeronima invited us to her home for tea. It must be one of the finest homes in Rio. When we gave the chauffeur her address, he said "Oh I know that house very well. I used to drive there to big receptions years ago".

It is a tall stone house with sweep and simplicity to the façade. Inside is a white hall with a big curving stairway and to the right a big dining room. To the left a long drawing room, at the back the small sitting room - all furnished in handsome Jaracanda-wood pieces and cabinets of family souvenirs and interesting family portraits on the walls, huge bowls of roses, and photographs of famous people on tables and the piano.

Tea was served at the big dining table and it was surely high tea - spread out on a gorgeous lace cloth all manner of scones, cakes, jams, sandwiches etc. Tea is a real meal in Rio and dinner is at ten. I said to my host, "I think I would eat tea and then just call it a day." "Oh no," he said, "I like dinner!" I'm sure he couldn't possibly imagine what a departure dinner at 10 would be for me.

After tea we went upstairs to visit the Baroness, the mother of Jeronima and Antonio. She is 92 years old and cannot leave her room because of a broken hip. She was sitting up as straight as an arrow doing her crochet. A tiny, stately figure with white hair done in a regal coiffure. We all kissed her fragile hand; it seemed the appropriate thing to do. We all spoke French and she told us about her days she was happy because she could have her game of bridge every evening and could listen to her radio (not the Voice of America!) and do her crochet. What a woman! No wonder her husband freed his slaves before others, no wonder her daughter is the moving spirit in all good works with such an example.

One day we were amused to hear from an English-speaking taxi driver. He said, "The women from the USA weep when they have to leave here. They never had it so good. Here sometimes they have two sometimes four servants. Home they never have even one. Here they can play cards from 11:00 AM till 11:00 PM". He must have known what he was talking about because he drove them and heard them talk. The ladies of his country didn't do it that way.

There was another foundation started by a talented poetess, Dona Ann Amelia de Mendonca. She had discovered that foreign students were at a loss in Rio, so she started an International House. There are rooms for men and women students at reduced rates, cafeterias and restaurants where food is good and not dear. Students come from all over South America as well as European countries, the USA and elsewhere.

Dona Ann Amelia is said to be Brazil's best poetess. She has translated many other poets of other languages. She has Edna St. Vincent Millay's poems. I asked her if it wasn't hard to do. She said, "Oh no it is like Shakespeare. It translates beautifully." My opinion of our Edna went up at once. Ann Amelia, as her friends call her, is at her office early each day and she runs an efficient business affair as well as a much-needed social service.

Each of these women has left the stamp of her personality on the life of the city and her times. It is impossible to imagine how they ever got along without the developments due to their individual efforts.

Mrs. Darci Vargas, the wife of the president, is a beautiful woman with wide blue eyes and a quiet dignity. Many years ago when her husband was not in politics she interested herself in the small boys.

As we all know, small boys everywhere often become fatherless. The mother has to leave home to earn the living and she has to have the help of the boys. In Rio school is compulsory. Most of the jobs the boys can do are after school hours; buses are crowded, no subways, no means of transport. So, Mrs. Vargas started a sort of Boys Town down in the heart of the busiest section of Rio. There are all manner of jobs nearby and there is a big school, so the boys live there and there are banking arrangements for them to give some of their earnings to their mothers and also they can save some as well. There is a big bulletin board with each boy's name and the amount he has in savings. The youngest is 10 and the oldest is 17. At that age, the boys go into compulsory military training.

The entire work is done by the boys themselves. The time we were there, lunch was just over, and the cafeteria was being cleaned by a group of youths about thirteen years old. They were scrubbing and scouring and disinfecting most expertly.

We were shown the Chapel and the music room. These boys have to have music so there were two pianos and many other instruments. Two boys were ill, so we visited the Infirmary and saw that they were being cared for. They have their dormitories, their swimming pools and baths, as well as soccer courts. In fact, everything.

We were invited to teas, luncheons and dinners and shown the kitchens with pride. Most modern! When they come to visit me, I shall take them elsewhere to see kitchens; mine hasn't had a new thing in 30 years.

We were invited to tea by a bachelor-girl. Her apartment was the last word! A huge window overlooking the beach, a built-in bed-divan, a built-in desk and bookcases, a tiny kitchenette and with it all, room for grand piano (for she is a musician). She served us tea in antique Portuguese fluted China cups that had been brought out by her forbears. Her table was spread with the lace cloth made on the family plantation after the designs of her ancestors, by women who were trained by her grandmother. She is coming to visit us soon, she said. I know she will find us old fashioned.

We were also invited to lunch at the Press Club. It is a tall, modern building and also the individual effort of one person. We were especially pleased that the card catalog in the indexing - that branch that of the modern world without which we could not wage war and get far in peace - that part was installed by a woman. It was done by Ignez Araujo.

They regaled us everywhere with special regional dishes that we couldn't praise enough. Our polite hosts would explain whose grandmother's recipe it was and then Ignez would say sweetly, as if to comfort us, "As for me I love that drug store on 57th St in New York. I love that cup of coffee and that big piece of chocolate cake!" She would smile so fetchingly, and I almost believed there was some truth in it.

We had lunch with one young couple, Dr. and Mrs. Belchior. The dessert was so good that I asked for the recipe and she gave it to me. I have it here for you. She said "It says, put through the sieve 10 times. That is not necessary. Just take two sieves and put it from one to the other." So that is the way to do it. We tried it and it was good.

Mrs. Belchior is a Boston girl. I was proud of her. She is a delicate ash blonde and has adapted herself so well to her adopted land you can't see where South America begins and where North America leaves off. One example is the little daughter. They have named her that beautiful name Laura. Her mother calls her as we do, and the child responds. Then when the grandmother calls her "Lah-oo-rah" as the as the Europeans say it and the child sweetly responds to both. Of course, this harmony is not due to one woman alone, it takes two. Together they have made a home both North American and South American - a true American home.

Several years ago, John Gunther wrote a book called Inside South America. He spent a year there gathering his material. As South America comprises some 24 countries, it meant that he spent about two weeks in each country. One of our South American students said to me, "It couldn't be inside South America, it must be inside John Gunther."

How true it is that we see what is reflected from ourselves. Ninteen days is too short a time to really know Rio. I tell only what I saw, and I speak from a woman's point of view. I know the difference from a man's.

My husband and I often sit side by side to do a painting. We use completely different colors. I leave out whatever I feel like leaving out and he puts in every twig and bush. Perhaps this review of our first visit to South America will be just as different. I speak for us women.

16

1955 - Opportunities for Women of the Middle East

Russell Family Archives

Editor's Introduction: Chloe was a member of many clubs including the Cosmopolitan Club in New York, and in Washington DC she was a member of the Washington Club (where she was the Chairman of the International Committee), the Woman Geographer's Club and the Women's City Club. The following account from her trip to with Will to the Middle East in 1955 could have been written as an address to any of these.

We often speak of the laws of the Medes and the Persians. It seems to hardly mean much anymore, but they were great laws. Theirs was a great civilization. Alexander the Great, in the most amazing feat of arms ever, went across great mountain ranges without wheels and defeated immense empires. It was a stupendous feat, and it is important that we properly estimate modern living in those countries to know at least something about their history.

What changes have gone on here in our country in the last 300 years are repeated there. We too had slavery, we also had almost no plumbing, we too had to go by stagecoach and in fear of robbers. We too had to build railroads across the country.

Our women also went to the wilder shores of the west. They did not crave the wide-open spaces. Genteel travel went by boat up and down the Mississippi to New Orleans. We hear of no American women braving the nomadic life with gusto. The English women seem different. There was a great urge amongst them to go to the far-off desert and live just like the Arabs. Several rich and titled women have gone out there and lived with the people. There are fascinating books about them. Freya Stark of our own day is one. Gertrude Bell is another.

What they wanted to do was to live like the men, between the sky and sand. There the men ran it all and the women were veiled and led most secluded lives.

Today we fly over those great mountain ranges and all we can do is dream of what it meant to go there by horse or donkey all those long years ago. In those day a stranger was likely to be shot on sight. The women lived a separate life. They wore the veil and were never seen by strangers. So a mass of silly stories were spread about them. The word sheik became almost synonymous with wickedness.

Mozart wrote "The Abduction from the Seraglio", Byron wrote, artists painted, the Arabian Nights was a great best-seller. And a shocker! World culture was preoccupied by things of the desert.

I remember in New York, when I was young I went into the home of the Vanderbilts on the Plaza.

The Cornelius Vanderbilt II Mansion
https://thegildedageera.blogspot.com/2012/07/the-cornelius-vanderbilt-ii-mansion-new.html

That beautiful little French chateau had been sold and was to be torn down, so for some charity or other it was opened to the public for a small sum. I went and wandered through it thinking that the taste of certain rich people was not too good, but I was impressed by one room. It was the "Den". There was reproduced a real Sheik's room complete with silk swags and cushions three feet deep and innumerable Persian rugs, brass coffee pots and even the mantle piece had a damask swag draped over it. The place was stuffy and much more appropriate to the windy tent of a Bedouin than to a little French chateau strangely sitting on Fifth Avenue, NY USA.

We were most interested, but it all seemed very far away at that time.

Today it is as near as Paris or London. Those countries have had as many changes as we have had. One comes down into modern airports. When we left Teheran a year ago in September a group of little boys boarded our plane for London. They were all wearing good looking London tweed top-coats and small caps like English school-boys. They were also speaking good English. I asked the stewardess who they were. She said, "Oh some Persian boys going back to school in England." I said, "Do they go alone like that?" she said "sure, why not?" So, you see the men begin young to go out in the world.

What of the women? They are as varied as we are. Some are rich and some poor. Some go veiled and some do not. Some live in towns, some in the country. Some read and write, some do not, some can read and write and will not do so. But all seem to know of their great history.

We cannot judge their wealth by the way they dress or how they look. Some of the richest are very public spirited and serious, like the Princess Firouz. Some wear the last word from Dior or Balenciaga. Other will look beautiful in brocades and chiffons in the old fashions.

Some of them will be veiled. They seem to be well contented with their own fashions.

The climate is important when it comes to dress. The entire country is mountainous and in places like Teheran the altitude is so high it is cold at night, but hot at noon. Winters are quite cold. They wear regional costumes that have become perfected by long generations of trial and error. They do dress for the seasons and the climate, and one is impressed by the perfection of the styling of garments. They go prepared for heat, sun, or wind.

Some Americans from Utah were sent out to bring our well-known "know how" to the farmers of Iran. The common people do not read or write so they should have gone to live in the villages and dressed in blue-jeans or overalls. They should have gone into the fields with the farmers and watched them run their irrigation ditches and water pumps, etc. After a study of the age-old ways, they could suggest something here or there from watching. Instead, they did not do that, they went to the cities and settled in the most modern hotels, spoke only English and lived more or less as in the US. Then they reported "These people are not interested in their hogs. They do not care about the yield of their corn. They listen to us tell them what to do to improve their crops and then pay no attention to what we say."

Someone said, and quite rightly, "Well, if you wanted to help the farmer in the U.S.A. you wouldn't go to Groton and start talking to the sons of the richest citizens.". That was what they did when they talked to those they felt were their equals.

The life out there has gone on for a long, long time and perhaps it is most luxurious and comfortable as well as most interesting from the point of view of sports and riding and living the way men have always liked to live outdoor lives. A most pleasant life with cushions and tents and easy clothing. The greatest library I have ever seen in a home was not in England, not in France, but out in Baghdad at the home of the then Prime Minister Fahdil Jamali. The library is largely Arabic but there are rooms of American books, English, French, etc. It covers the entire walls of the first floor of a large modern house. It was the library of the father of M. Jamali who was a great Sheik and the head of the Mosque. The family was Persian about 1000 years ago and before that they came from India about 2000 years ago – so said Fahdil.

I hope this very brief resume of what goes on behind the walls of the people of those lands will help us to imagine the life of the women. Some of them live just like ourselves, but with one big difference, they know about their ancient past and are proud of it. Sometimes I hear people ask, "What is your background?" The English people laugh at Americans for their preoccupation with their ancestors. We can tell about some parts of our history of about 100 years but little more. I believe it may be good in some ways. We have lost our fears. If an American woman loses her head over some man, she does not lose it in reality, but the woman of the middle east can expect to die for it if she oversteps in any way the sacred rules for women's behavior. Their families see to it. They are judge and executioner. The women know their traditions and they respect them.

Lebanon was the first of those countries to become Christian. The blood of the Martyrs is so potent there. We were taken high up on the mountain, and it was explained that the village had been converted to Christianity very early, then came the Turks. They took over the village and made the ruling that the men should foreswear Christ. They refused so thus were slaughtered. All of them to the number of 900. After that everyone became Christian and the Turks had to leave the country. Being Christian, the women were not obliged to veil the face, and were considered the equal of the men. We hardly realize our privileges not only as Americans but also as Christians.

Women there have been educated and have traveled everywhere in the world. So Madam Chamoun, the wife of the President of Lebanon, told me that she receives letters very often from men in all the desert countries asking her to find them a Lebanese wife. "A Lebanese woman can go everywhere with her husband, and he can be proud of her" was what they wrote. If you meet the wives of the ambassadors from Iraq or Iran you will find that they are from Lebanon. They are refined and gentle and well educated.

The modesty of the women was refreshing. Of course they have sort of topsy turvey ideas from our point of view. I have seen a woman in full purdah toss up her skirts and relieve herself quite publicly behind a tree near a highway. She was not an educated woman, but her head was covered so she felt herself as modest as necessary.

Their manners are slow and respectful and the poorest have great dignity and sweetness towards strangers. There is a well of woman power that has not been tapped and the women are so willing. They take picture of a pullover from Paris and with infinite patience they will plot the stitches until they have a copy. Then the copy is passed around the whole country until all the people are wearing the latest in Paris pullovers.

In one village the doctor's wife could read and write so she sent to Paris for a needlework magazine, and she would pick out a style and knit it, then give hers to the village women who could copy it. How hard it was without the blessing of reading. This is something we can develop or leave it for the Reds to exploit.

About thirty years ago, one of the students at Teacher's College was talking to me about his home in Iran or Persia. He complained that it was so hard for him because his wife could not read or write so the news from his home was sketchy and unsatisfactory. "When I go home, I intend to see that she learns. That all our women learn." That was in 1932. I met him last year and with him was another wife. This wife was well educated and telling me about her little boy who wanted to have his horse in Teheran, but it is too expensive, just like any American city and all the little boys here wanting to have their horse and dreaming of Hop-a-Long.

It is wholesome before we go far examining a foreign country from the point of view of their women and education and we try to imagine what makes them do as they do. Many Arabs live here in our country, and they enjoy the plumbing and all of our ways, but the ones who chose to live on the desert want to live between the sky and the sand using as few man-made articles as possible. They want their rugs and plenty of them. They want their veils and capes and tents and they feel great need for their horses. Their water systems and their wells and gardens, but our shoes and our clothes and so on do not fill them with envy.

They have only to look up and there are ruins of some ancient city with buildings that cannot be reproduced today, so they admire the pictures of our skyscrapers but reserve the thought, "Yes, but have you seen Isfahan?"

The same student talked to me about his visit to NY where he came to receive an honorary degree. He described his visit to Ireland. He said "when the Irish people learned that a man from Iran would land at Shannon Airport they came to meet me and insisted on taking me for a visit to their homes. You see the Irish and the Iranians stem from the same sources long ago. I was perfectly at home. The way the Squire in Ireland lives is the way we live in the country in Iran.

Tehran is a very cosmopolitan city. When I was lost and wandering in the Russian neighborhood, I saw a small boy on a cycle and asked him in French to tell me how to go home. He told me very well. He was one of the little carpet weavers.

The women are not even allowed to have anything to do with washing the rugs. This is a most interesting process. The finished rugs are put in the river and the stream allowed to run over them. The colors glow like gorgeous gems and the water runs and runs. When finished, the rugs are spread out on the rocks in the sun to dry. While watching the process, Mrs. Samii, who accompanied me, said. "See those white things in the fields there?" I saw bits and hunks of a white sort of chalk substance. Those are human bones, she explained. "This was a great battlefield about 2,000 years ago" I gazed at a thigh bone sticking out of the hillside and did truly feel that I had arrived very late in this country.

How about the little girls? They weave not, neither do they spin. It seems to be protection, but it is also means the men control the purse. The little girls are very pretty and at birth their ears are pierced, and ting gold earrings attached. Even the very poor manage to get gold earrings for their girl babies. They seemed to always be dressed in pretty cotton printed dresses with the Chador over their heads.

I visited a village belonging to the Princess Firouz. She is public spirited, and her villages are supposed to be models. Outside of the walls was a new school with a large playground. School was not in session, but the interpreter said it was as good as any school in the USA. When we entered the village, we saw the women gathered around the Joub. This is a wide ditch that runs down the main street of the Persian villages or towns. The underground water is apparently tapped from two separate sources. In the Joub it was clear, but in the sewage ditches the water was milky showing that it came from a glacial source. The mountains are high, many as high as 12,000 feet. So the water races in the Joub and no one seems he worse for the washing of the baby or the fruits or vegetables all in the same place. It is lucky they are accustomed to their own germs.

Here at last I found the male sex in a bad way for a line of little boys stood against the wall and wept. They did not bawl or howl, just wept, streams of tears with runny noses and no one notices them at all. I could hardly bear it I wanted to begin with some paper handkerchiefs and console them. I asked what ailed all those poor little boys. "They are boys. We protect the girls. The boy has to learn to become a man." And on we went leaving the boys to become men!

The homes in the village were like the ones in the Bible, all swept and garnished. One room with a mantle shelf and fireplaces. On the shelf of one house was a samovar and cups or glasses and spoons. Some had handsome Persian rugs on the smooth dirt floor and in the corner would be a sort of bundle, the bed tied up in a cotton printed or handwoven cover. Some had a cradle hanging from a rafter. As we passed through the village the little girls ran along with us skipping on their tiny bare feet and smiling most beguilingly. Perfect little beauties, contented and happy.

One woman invited me to her house. We entered through a small Persian garden. It was laid out around a pool and there was a well with a very odd-looking water bucket. The garden had two trees at each end. One was full of beautiful pomegranates. They make the sweet grenadine with them. The other was hanging with big, luscious-looking nectarines. There were flowers of all kinds blooming grandly. The well bucket was interesting and the woman seeing that I looked at it began to laugh and told the interpreter to tell me that it was made from an old truck tire from the USA!

She then led us to the WC. I asked the interpreter why she did so. He answered that she wanted to show me how clean it was with no smell. How it is done is one more of those Arabic secrets.

The school for the Gendarmes was interesting. I went there expecting to see only men, but the teacher was a woman so according to Arab customs a woman may learn from a woman, so there was one woman there. She was a prize pupil and wrote the complicated Arabic script and read easily and fluently. She was the mother of six children and said there was no one to teach the women of her village to read and write so she would try to do it.

The class for midwives was interesting. About seven women were there, the teachers had been trained in England, or France or the USA. Some of the women who are doing important work in their country were invited to meet me. Their names may be interesting, and their work:

Miss Taguis Obramian – Supervisor of the teaching of the Gendarmes
Mrs Torran Aclam – Supervisor of the Teacher Training
Dr Kazemi – Physician employed by the Dept. of Labor
Mrs. Marian Daftari – Assistant to the Home Economics Section
Mrs. Saidi Neginni – Midwifery Supervisor
Mrs Zahra Samii – Home Extension of Agriculture

Devoted, good looking, charming and well dressed in western fashions, these women love their country and all they want is to be allowed to work, but as I have said the men like to work too and if possible be paid, so the women are encouraged to stay home and knit.

The women all talked to me of their fears of Russia. They said over and over that if they came Christ would die and they all believe in God and in Christ. Their only difference to us is that they believe he was just like Mohammed, a great prophet.

One perfectly beautiful and well-educated woman talked to me about our marriage customs. She said, "my parents loved me so much that they selected my husband for me. I did not see him until a few days before the wedding, then he passed by my house and a friend pointed him out. I looked and was filled with joy. I felt God had just opened up the sky and dropped him down just for me." She had always been most happy with him, and yet he died suddenly. She wept and said "Oh I am doing all I can to get permission to go to the USA with my children. I do so fear Russia."

They were interested in our education for girls. Somehow, they had an idea that everything was "Specialize". They seemed surprised when I told them that our girls learn quite a lot before they decide what to specialize in. They have just plain learning.

Now briefly about Iraq. The woman wear the Purdah on the streets, but not in their home. Visiting the Mosque, we met several woman coming towards us with pretty ankles and patent leather high heeled pumps. As they passe me they said softly and sweetly "Good Afternoon!" I had a brief moment when I could see a bit of the surprise and excitement so many people feel about veiled women. All you see is a figure enveloped in a black cape, one eye shows, or both eyes, or no eyes at all. So the foot and the ankle is what you judge by. If there is a gold bangle or a Paris shoe it does start you wondering what the rest of the girl looks like.

I was invited to a tea at one home, a most modern stone house with a garden and garage, etc. When I entered the servant brought me a small cup of the heavy coffee and there was a bright fire burning in the fireplace. My hostess said the thing she so well remembered at my home in New York was that I had a fire in my fireplace also. Everything in the house was most comfortable and clean and well cared for. Tea was served in the dining room and the table was covered with a long, most beautifully embroidered cloth. I admired it and the hostess seemed much pleased. "I made it all myself" she said. She had been living in Paris for some time and sewing seems to come naturally to these women, so she designed and made this beautiful thing while she had some leisure time. Also the cakes were made by her and delicious.

The other guests began to come in big Cadillacs or other cars, some of them official. I was so interested that they were all important in some way to the life of the city or the country. They all signed my book, and their names fascinate me:

My hostess – Mrs Asma Kadim – Inspectress of Schools

Mrs. Asia Tawfeek Wahley - Head of Women's guild of Child Welfare

Mrs. Adeeba Ibrahim Rifart - Principal of the Elementary Teachers Training College

Mrs. Melila Hakim - Principal of the Secondary School for Girls

Dr Sanina Amin Zaki – Royal Hospital – Trained in Russia

Adahmiza Sellex

The women are seldom seen on the street. They go and come in cars or closed sorts of Phaetons or on donkeys. The little white donkeys run down the sidewalks and feel most at home there. Sometimes women are the riders but mostly men or boys ride. The women stay at home, but the little girls can be seen running to school every morning. They dress in little uniforms of dark blue pleated skirts and a white middy blouse. All have bobbed hair and wear a ribbon to tie their top lock. The color of the ribbon tells what class they belong in. They all carry a board under one arm. The board is painted black, and they write on it with chalk. They have a cord that goes over the shoulder so that they can run without fear of dropping the board.

Their schools are very crowded so there are not enough seats, and each group of children has a pile of mats and they take their mat and sit down on the floor.

In Baghdad the little boys fared better it seemed to me, but in one class the littlest girl took over the head of the line. She dawdled till the whole class was behind her, then began to lead the dance. The children were full of imagination and did one dance as airplanes and wheeled and dipped and buzzed most realistically.

Some political thing had just transpired at that time and one small boy said to me, "I can't like Americans when they do bad for us and good for the Jews." He said it sadly – almost tearfully. So the children are all in it out there.

Mrs Jamali, the wife of the Prime Minister, asked my husband to help her obtain sewing machines for an adult education project she was running. The machines went out at once and she wrote me a letter telling me that the women were doing a big job sewing.

I met the woman who makes the uniforms for Pan Am and the Howard Johnson Company. She told me that some of the work was done in Baghdad and some in Lebanon. So at least a few women can earn money even if they cannot read or write.

Their clothing is also something that has come down to them through a myriad of generations. It is perfected for their way of life and their culture. The ladies may lay aside their purdah when they enter, but the men lay aside their European dress. They put on the head dress and their robe and settle down to solid comfort.

Also they have their cafes. Every corner has a café and the men are there smoking their odd narghiles. The pipe rests on the floor and is a big sort of gourd-shaped affair with a long hose. The hose has a removable mouthpiece and each man brings his own. Thus the pipes are kept in a row on the shelf of the favorite café and the man drops in any time, fixes his mouthpiece and has a good time with the men. I thought of the bit in the Bible where the good woman sees to it that her husband sits with the wise men at the gates.

In Iraq, the woman are educated if the family is wealthy. It is still that way for the educated are the wealthy and the people interested in learning are the educated. They seize the opportunities for learning.

Now for the women of Lebanon. As I have said they have had all the advantages of Christianity for ages but they too are all kinds and also deeply imbued with the age of their customs. In the garden of a friend a man was working among the plants. He wore a drab garment made with sort of Jodphur leggings and a very full padded seat made with many gores. His shirt was long sleeved, and over it he wore a sort of quilted vest. He was stooping down in a sort of squat position and maneuvering the water in a ditch. My friend said, "That old costume he wears is something special, designed just for the job. It doesn't look much, but it is very traditional. We call it his droopy-drawers."

That is the way with most of the clothes the people wear. They are handed-down designs. Also the same friend said, "Everything these people do has a good reason."

The women are intelligent and good looking. Good sewers and knitters, but just as elsewhere the men manage to do most of the money-making jobs.

The women take to new ways with zest. I visited a small home economics center way up in the mountains. A little woman was running it. She had been trained in Paris and had married a Frenchman. She was trying to teach by demonstration entirely because of the illiteracy of the women. She gave me a demonstration of a way to prepare the eggplant. I will prepare some for you some day. She was a very good teacher indeed.

Madame Chamoun, the wife of the President, told me a little bit when I talked to her and told her about the demonstration. She said that in Lebanon there are 29 ways of preparing eplant so there is a saying that if your wife asks you "What shall we eat?" you should divorce her. She should know enough to know at least one of the ways of fixing eggplant!

The houses of Lebanon are very good. They are made of stone and the floors are marble. One man told me, "When we want a house, we just go out and hack it out of the hillside." They believe in the "Do It Yourself" idea.

The country lies along the sea and is the size of the State of Connecticut. There are two parallel ranges of mountains, the Lebanons and the Anti-Lebanons, and in between lies a fertile valley. They tell us it is the original Garden of Eden.

In Lebanon, in Beirut, the principal of one of the girls' schools asked me to speak to her pupils. When I arrived, she took me first to her sitting room and gave me the usual hot, sugared, strong coffee.

When we were comfortably seated, she asked me a bit nervously what I was going to tell the girls, then without giving me the time to reply she said, "I thought it would be good if you told them about President Eisenhower." I agreed and said that I would be glad to do so.

Then she asked me, "What had you intended to say?" I proceeded to tell her, and she seemed much excited and said "Oh, tell them that. They do so need a buildup." So, I talked the way I had intended and added something about the President and afterwards she was most enthusiastic and said, "you have build them up so they will never come down."

The girls were so charming to me. They followed me out and insisted that I pose with them so here are their pictures.

All they need in Lebanon is more schools and more teachers and the people are so refined, they will do the rest.

Following the trip to the Middle East described above Chloe and WFR (second from left) traveled through Egypt.
Russell Family Archives

www.ingramcontent.com/pod-product-compliance
Lightning Source LLC
Chambersburg PA
CBHW071812160426
43209CB00032B/1937/J